MW00769140

Have you ever wondered how immigrants, many of whom can't even speak English, come to America and own their own homes or businesses within a short period of time?

What do they know that the rest of us don't know?

This book answers those questions and gives a foundation for *Making It in America.*

MAKING IT IN AMERICA

MAKING IT IN AMERICA

What Immigrants Know and Americans Have Forgotten

MARCIA A. STEELE

Maxmar

Designed by Mori Studio

Printed in the United States of America.

04 03 02 01 00   6 5 4 3 2 1

Library of Congress Catalog Card Number: 99-684-36

ISBN 1-893232-07-7

DEDICATION

I dedicate this book to my mother, who taught me everything I needed to know about life and "making it" under any circumstance, and to my sister Laurice, who helped me regain my focus.

It is my sincere wish that this book will stimulate at least one idea, desire, or dream that launches you on a new beginning that will be both successful and fulfilling.

TABLE OF CONTENTS

ACKNOWLEDGMENTS

I would like to thank the following: In particular, friend and editor Steve Cohn for his encouragement and insights, and emotional support, all of which helped make this possible; Mark LeBlanc, friend and business advisor, for always being on the team; and Janet Boyce, my research analyst extraordinaire.

I am also greatful to my general advisors and advocates Emma Morris, Brian Shaver, Michelle Rousseau, Rudolph Bancroft, Amy Swisher, and Tim Hurson. Thanks to Vincent Paribello, Dr. Shirley Garrett, Helen Cleaveland, Diane James, Gene Cloud, Gwen Dickerson, June Cline, Myra McElhaney, Jean Houston Shore, Alon Kvashny, Dave Gunby, Winfried Laane, Natalie Potter, Attorney Valrie Abrahams, and Barry Moreno.

THE PLACE

Why we come.

Chapter 1

WHAT IMMIGRANTS KNOW

(AND SOME OF US HAVE FORGOTTEN)

Have you ever wondered how immigrants, many of whom can't even speak English, come to America and own their own homes and businesses within a short period of time? How do they do it while others—with presumably more advantages—struggle just to make ends meet?

What do they know that the rest of us don't know?

This book addresses these very questions. And although I didn't set out to write a "how to" book, that is what this has turned out to be.

From the very start I'd like to say that not all immigrants have learned these principles, and certainly not all Americans have forgotten them. However, there are sufficient similarities within each group to warrant several generalities.

This book is neither a documentary account nor an in-depth study of any one thing, so the chapters can be read in any order, though reading them sequentially is probably still best.

What you will find in this book is a collection of simple ideas, strategies, and common-sense know-how that many immigrants have used to create success.

I will show you how the ability to make choices helped immigrants come to America and live better lives, and how Americans can use their examples to help themselves make better choices.

I'll share with you the experience that has allowed immigrants to leave everything behind to follow and achieve their dreams, and how they make it happen with a simple phrase—"if it's to be, it's up to me."

Together we'll explore the framework and strategies immigrants have used to become successful in this land of opportunity. But most importantly, you'll discover that these simple, easy-to-apply concepts are open to all: immigrants and Americans alike.

Let me share with you how this project began.

In 1992, I found myself in a quandary. From the outside it looked as if I had a pretty good life. I was a successful software consultant traveling the world for both business and pleasure. I lived in a comfortable four-bedroom, three-bathroom house in the northeast suburbs of Atlanta. I had lots of friends and a very active social life. Yet I was miserable. My life was a shambles on the inside.

My job was neither fulfilling nor challenging. I was bored working for a company whose market share was shrinking by the day. My stock options weren't worth the paper they were written on and I was deeply in debt. I wasn't exactly having a good time. Dilbert would say, "Press F1 for help. Hey, it's an application form for a job at McDonald's."

I knew things had to change, but I didn't know where to start. Should I change jobs and go to Oracle, PeopleSoft or Manugistics, as many of my friends were doing? Or should I quit my complaining, stay, and try to force myself to be satisfied and grateful for all that I had? With each passing day my morale began to match the company's sales—getting lower by the minute.

I played with the idea of starting my own business, but I needed "seed money." The company was laying off employees, and the severance package it was offering would have come in handy. I discussed the possibilities of this with a good friend who was a company vice president. I distinctly remember the tone in his voice when he said, "Are you crazy? You are black, female and good. We want people like you. Your chances of making a layoff list are between slim and nil! If you want out, you'd better plan on quitting."

I was caught in a Catch-22. I couldn't stay but I didn't know where to go or what to do. I'd had enough of forecasting, warehouse management, customer service, and computer implementations to last me a lifetime. But I didn't think I was qualified to do anything else.

I wanted a fresh start but I was afraid. What if I failed? What if I lost everything? What would people say?

Then, the most interesting thing happened. In discussing my dilemma with friends, I found out that I was not alone. We all felt trapped to an extent and felt a great deal of uncertainty about our futures. We had come eyeball to eyeball with the truth. We were caught in a chasm.

I realized then that the biggest challenge facing us in America today is not global competition or technology, but rather complacency and fear! Half of us are complacent with the status quo, and the other half live in fear of losing the status quo.

And as long as we are caught in that Catch-22, we will never have the passion, the drive, or the guts to break free, to discover new frontiers, or forge new and better tomorrows. What my friends and I were experiencing were the early signs of a deadly virus that, if not stopped, could quickly reduce this great nation to a second-tier world power.

I began to reflect on previous beginnings—times where the status quo was challenged and new frontiers were discovered. I recalled my own experience of "coming to America" at age 20, and the floodgates of my mind literally flew open. All the feelings, the excitement and the fears, the insights and the similarities came rushing in. America was indeed a country of new beginnings! Particularly, a country of new adult beginnings. This is perhaps the single thing we most have in common:

Either our parents, our grandparents, or we ourselves came to America looking for new beginnings.

I realized then that I needn't be afraid. I already knew everything I needed to know. I needed only to recall what I had obviously forgotten.

After all, I was no stranger to change. I had made a huge change in coming to America some thirty years earlier and had survived quite well. I bought my first piece of property within three years of arriving here, a second piece one year later, and my first home two years after that.

So was it something special about me back then that caused these things to happen? No, I don't think so. There is nothing I know that others don't already know or cannot learn.

Like everyone else, I've had my ups and downs and some of the downs have been way down. So, I write not from a position of arrogance but rather from a position of recognizing how little credit we give ourselves. I believe we each have within us what it takes to acquire our American dream. Unfortunately, what we know subconsciously doesn't always make it into our consciousness. And our power lies not in what we know, but in how we use what we know.

I knew that if I didn't make a change, I would regret it for the rest of my life. I simply needed to recall the things I had done to survive and thrive in past times of change. I had to make them part of my consciousness. I had to move my power from my subconscious mind into my conscious behavior.

I needed to also recall that success is a very personal thing; it means different things to different people. And that only I had the right and the responsibility to determine what success looked and felt like to me.

I believe that, for most people, success and feelings of accomplishment come from both financial gain and heart gain. I was enjoying a relatively comfortable financial gain, but my heart was no longer engaged. At work I was simply going through the motions. And I wasn't being true to my employer or myself. I needed to find new challenges and new frontiers; I needed to feel passionate about my life's contributions.

What I needed to do was to touch base with my immigrant roots, and continue on a journey of new beginnings.

If you want to *Make It in America*, remember . . .

- The biggest challenge facing us is not global competition or technology, but ***complacency and fear***.

- America is a country with a history of new beginnings.

- Power lies not in what we know, but in how we ***use*** what we know.

One reason many people are not living their dreams is that there is something they are trained to honor more than their dreams:

THE COMFORT ZONE

Chapter 2

WE ARE ALL IMMIGRANTS

(FROM SOMEWHERE)

Thousands of years ago, long before the American Revolution and the settlement of the colonies, this land was home to only one race, the American Indian, or Native American. Quite by accident, Christopher Columbus, an Italian sailing under the Spanish flag, stumbled upon the jewel we know as America.

America can be described as a one-of-a-kind jewel. Jewels are usually considered to be precious, multifaceted, brilliant stones that can withstand a fair amount of wear and tear yet can shatter if not handled properly.

Let's look at our unique jewel.

If there is one overriding factor that marks the United States as different from other nations, it is the principle that all people are created equal. The tragedy brought on by ethnic and racial intolerance throughout the world is proof of the precious anomaly that exists in what we call America.

Consider all the ethnic wars and strife that have torn apart nations and peoples. We have seen nation turn against nation, race against race, religion against religion, in Germany, Russia, Czechoslovakia, Ireland, Vietnam, Bosnia, Iraq, Indonesia, and numerous places in Africa, to name just a few.

Yet in America, those same races and religions live relatively peaceably side-by-side. The constitution and laws that form the framework for that peace have withstood the wear and tear of daily struggles. Yet, like any precious stone, America is subject to being shattered if it is not handled properly.

The constitution of the United States begins: "We the people of the United States . . ." Yet, the United States is not and never has been made up of any single group of people. It is made up of a multifaceted, multiracial group of immigrants from every corner of the earth and from every walk of life. Describing America, Walt Whitman said, "Here is not merely a nation, but a teeming nation of nations."

Thankfully, arriving immigrants didn't abandon their ethnic traditions when they arrived in America. Each ethnic group held on to its traditions and customs, its foods, and festivals. And it is these differences that have added spice, genius, and brilliance to this mosaic.

The strategy that has taken America to its top-of-the-world leadership in education, space exploration, and commerce is nothing short of brilliant: It simply offers its people freedom and choice, not control and power.

The 1953 United States Commission on Immigration and Naturalization said,

> Our growth as a nation has been achieved, in large measure, through the genius and industry of immigrants of every race and from every quarter of the world. The story of their pursuit of happiness is the saga of America. Their brains and their brawn helped to settle our land, to advance our agriculture, to build our industries, to develop our commerce, to produce new inventions and in general, to make us the leading nation that we now are.

The children of immigrants are doubly blessed as they walk the fine line between sometimes opposing cultures. They, their friends, their music, and their dress are all-American. Yet as children of immigrants, they are raised socializing with their immigrant parents and their parents' friends. With such strong influences, these immigrant-descended, second-generation Americans identify so much with their Italian, Korean, Jamaican, Brazilian, or other ethnic heritage that they are often taken to be immigrants themselves.

Maybe that is why second-generation Americans are often seen as more successful than their third- and fourth-generation counterparts. Maybe it's because, like their parents, they are blessed with the fresh heritage of both the old and the new.

Herman Melville's words are as true today as they were in the 1840s when he wrote,

> We are the heirs of all time, and with all nations we divide our inheritance. On this Western Hemisphere, all tribes and peoples are forming into one federated whole; and there is a future which shall see the estranged children of Adam restored as to the old hearth-stone, Eden . . . . The seed is sown, and the harvest must come.

Yes. We are all immigrant nomads in one form or another. We are all immigrant heirs to this treasure, this jewel.

If you want to *Make It in America*, remember . . .

- America, like a jewel, is precious and multifaceted, yet can shatter if not handled properly.

- The growth of America has been achieved, in large measure, through the genius and industry of immigrants of every race.

- We are the heirs of all time, and with all nations we divide our inheritance.

"This land was made for you and me."
—Woody Guthrie

Chapter 3

FRIEND OR FOE

(CAN YOU HANDLE THE TRUTH?)

Throughout our history, Americans have both welcomed and hated their immigrant roots. Back in 1923, an anti-immigration song called *"Close the Gates!"* was published in New York. The lyrics went like this:

> *Close the gates of our nation,*
> *lock them firm and strong!*
> *Before this mob from Europe,*
> *shall drag our colors down.*

Even today, recent changes in immigration law pose real threats to the procedural rights of foreign-born persons in the United States. Pro-immigration and ethnic advocacy groups depict U.S. immigration policy as nativist and brutal. Even Amnesty International lumps attacks on American immigration policies together with its critique of dictatorships.

Congress itself adds to the debate as to whether immigrants should be welcomed or feared. On one hand, it granted amnesty to millions of illegal aliens, yet on the other hand, it enlarged the Border Patrol to the point that it is now the government's largest domestic uniformed service.

Which side is right? Is the immigrant friend or foe to America? Can both be right?

In this book, we focus on those who enter this country legally. The vast majority of those who come here from other countries come legally. It is those immigrants whom we speak about in these pages.

I believe that virtually all Americans treasure this country's immigrant heritage and ethnic diversity, and that most welcome immigrants as long as they pay their own way, don't take jobs away from other Americans or go on welfare, don't force bilingual education or get special breaks, and don't break the law. Guess what? Immigrants to America feel the same way.

Let's examine some of the facts and answer some of the questions.

First, where are immigrants coming from and why do they come?

Driven by hardships at home, and drawn by the promise of economic opportunities, millions and millions of immigrants have disembarked in various American ports. Between 1880 and 1930, over 500,000 Italians and more than 700,000 Irish arrived through Boston.

The New York Ellis Island Immigration Station opened its doors to the world on Friday, January 1, 1892. Millions came, as if in response to the Emma Lazarus poem inscribed on a bronze tablet on the Statue of Liberty: *Give me your tired, your poor, your huddled masses yearning to breathe free, . . . Send these, the homeless, tempest-tossed, to me: I lift my lamp beside the golden door.*

Between 1892 and 1954 over 12 million immigrants passed through Ellis Island. The majority came from England, Ireland, Italy, Germany, Russia, and Poland. The book *Ellis Island, Gateway to the American Dream* by Pamela Kilian and Pamela Reeves (Crescent Books, 1991) reports, "Four out of ten Americans can trace their heritage via Ellis Island."

However, not all immigrants came as a matter of choice. Beginning in 1619, when the captain of a Dutch man-of-war sold a handful of captives to settlers of Jamestown, until well into the 18th century, Africans were captured and sold as slaves here in America. They, too, were immigrants, though not voluntarily.

After the slaves were freed during the Civil War, anti-immigrant legislation in the early 20th century made sure that black people were not as welcome here as immigrants from other lands.

Things opened up with the Immigration and Nationality Act of 1952. It eliminated race as a bar to immigration, thus making all races eligible for naturalization. It also eliminated discrimination by gender and revised the "national origins" quota system, giving instead a quota preference to "skilled aliens whose services are urgently needed in the United States" and to relatives of U.S. citizens and aliens.

When Communist Fidel Castro came to power in Cuba in 1959, Cubans began to seek asylum here in the United States. Between 1959 and 1962, over 200,000 came, the majority choosing to settle in Miami, Florida, geographically close to their beloved homeland.

During 1996, the most recent year for which we have records, the largest share of immigrants came from North America (37%), followed by Asia (34%) and Europe (16%). African immigrants comprised only 6% of the total. Mexico was the leading source country with 163,572, or 18% of all immigrants.

Why the fear and resentment of immigrants?

Early in the 1900s, the restrictionist movement warned that the influx of "inferior" races from Asia and southern Europe would soon destroy "Anglo-Saxon America." Nativists preyed on the country's fear of outsiders and broadcast messages that were virulently anti-Catholic, anti-Semitic, and anti-Asian. The descendants of immigrants have tried to counter those fears by noting the contributions that immigrants have made to this great nation.

In 1996, New York Mayor Rudolph W. Giuliani, a descendant of Italian immigrants, gave an address to the Kennedy School of Government in Cambridge, Massachusetts. I found his words both enlightening and comforting.

The anti-immigrant movement in America endangers the single most important reason for American greatness, namely the renewal, reformation and reawakening that's provided by the continuous flow of immigrants who are seeking to create better lives for themselves and their families . . . and who succeed in doing so.

In his speech, Mayor Giuliani shared some interesting insights and observations.

- In New York City, foreign-born males are 10 percent more likely to be employed than native-born males. Foreign-born women are employed at the same rate as native-born women.

- In New York City, immigrants own businesses in higher percentages than other Americans. And immigrants in New York City are 10 percent *less* likely to be on public assistance than are native-born Americans.

- Nationwide, immigrants account for 50 percent of all professors of engineering.

- Immigrants account for 21 percent of all U.S. physicians and are net contributors to our economy.

Giuliani recalled that in 1989, Flushing, New York, was a community in serious economic distress. Stores were closing and businesses were fleeing the neighborhood. Today, we find a very different story. Stores are occupied; streets are crowded and teeming with activity. There are new restaurants, businesses, manufacturing, and even a new hotel. The mayor emphasized that this economic renaissance did not come from government subsidies. It came from the hard work of people striving to build better lives. Many of these people were born in China, Vietnam, India, Korea, and other countries. In other words, they're immigrants . . . new Americans.

This kind of success is seen repeatedly throughout New York City. There is a thriving Russian-American community in Brighton Beach. West Indian immigration helped rebuild neighborhoods in Brooklyn. In Jackson Heights, Latin Americans, South Americans, and people from the Caribbean have created a dynamic community. And strong immigration from Ireland is revitalizing Woodlawn and other areas of the Bronx.

Giuliani added that in New York, the richest and most successful city in the country, more than 28 percent of the population is foreign born. And, according to the Kennedy School of Government, this immigrant-rich city sends to Washington, D.C., about $11 billion more each year than it receives in return. Much of the money that New York City contributes to other states is created by immigrants and by the children of immigrants.

And the contributions of immigrants extend beyond big cities like New York and San Francisco to include such places as Atlanta, Georgia. An *Inc.* magazine writer, Marc Ballon, in an article entitled "Melting Pot," noted that according to the 1980 census, the population of Chamblee, Georgia, a suburb of Atlanta, was 90 percent white. And the influx of immigrants went largely unnoticed—for a while.

By 1992, that lily-white community was transformed into a kind of multiethnic, multilingual melting pot. Sadly, it became a poster city for xenophobia and economic backwardness. Tensions became so great that the chief of police was overheard saying at a city council meeting, "Your problems will continue until these people go back where they came from." He didn't mean Atlanta.

Thankfully, many immigrant entrepreneurs stepped in. They went about quietly renovating large unsightly patches of Chamblee. Today, a thriving Don Taco Mexican restaurant stands on the site of what was an abandoned International House of Pancakes restaurant. The Summit National Bank, partly founded by Chinese-Americans, occupies a new three-story building on the site of an old junkyard. And the Orient Center, a $2-million development project featuring Chinese,

Vietnamese, and Malaysian restaurants, has supplanted a run-down Chevrolet dealership.

Chamblee now has an estimated 100 immigrant-owned businesses, from Vietnamese restaurants to Chinese-language bookstores and Mexican record shops. These new enterprises have rescued distressed properties and fattened the tax rolls. Chamblee Community Development Director Paige Perkins says, "If the immigrants hadn't come, Chamblee would look like a bombed-out 1950s American dream, complete with empty strip malls and abandoned buildings."

Over and over again, the facts support the claim that immigrants are hard workers and good neighbors. The FannieMae Foundation reports that immigrants are becoming homeowners at a more rapid rate than those born here, and this trend is expected to provide a powerful boost to the country's housing market. The report found that in 1980, 22 percent of U.S. immigrants owned homes. By 1990, home ownership among this group had leapt to 47 percent.

The report said that between 1980 and 1995, the number of immigrant homeowners increased by 1.4 million, and projected that by 2010 that number would grow by 50 percent to 2.2 million homeowners. According to the FannieMae report, at least 51 percent of the foreign-born U.S. population are homeowners, compared to 68 percent for Americans born here.

So back to our original question, is the immigrant friend or foe? The facts overwhelmingly support the claim that legal immigrants revitalize and reinvigorate the culture and economy of our cities and states and, as such, are friends. Just look at the popularity of and interest in ethnically different offerings, from Thai and Mexican restaurants to Celtic and reggae music.

The truth is that America is an immigrant nation with a long, proud tradition of inclusion and diversity.

If you want to *Make It in America*, remember. . .

- Immigrants are drawn by the promise of economic opportunities.

- Immigrants rescue many communities in serious economic distress and revitalize and reinvigorate the culture and economy of our cities.

- Immigrants provide a powerful boost to the country's housing market.

The power of America, like that of light, lies in the spectrum of its many colors.

Chapter 4

WHY AMERICA?
(AND NOT TAHITI OR CANADA?)

I am, like many, an immigrant by birth, an American by choice.

It's been many years since I proudly accepted citizenship in this country of freedom and opportunity. As I look back on my experience and that of many others, I see some interesting parallels.

Let me continue to answer the question, "Why do immigrants come to America?"

It is because America is where ambition meets possibilities.

In other countries you may have the ambition but not the opportunities. Or your opportunities may be limited because of your gender, religion, or ethnic background. In some countries you could have the ambition, the opportunity, the money and the right everything, yet you are still limited by what the government will permit you to do.

At the core of American success is its ability to attract ambitious people. America is not successful because Americans are ambitious; it is successful because it attracts ambitious people.

Let me repeat that. America is not successful because Americans are ambitious; it is successful because it attracts ambitious people.

Ambitious immigrants had the qualities for success in them before they arrived here. What they lacked was opportunity.

Take Elena Khazanova, the first foreign-born valedictorian at Columbia University in recent memory. She arrived in South Burlington, Vermont, in 1991, just months before the collapse of the Soviet Union. Elena barely knew her father because her parents had divorced when she was a child. However, when he and his new family obtained permission to emigrate from Odessa to the United States, he offered to take her with them. It was a decision which meant she would have to give up her Soviet citizenship and any hopes of returning to Russia.

"I had to struggle with my feelings in order to follow my mind, and at the same time that was the struggle between the past and the future," Elena said. "In Russia I did not see an opportunity for progress in my own life, and that is why I decided to come to the U.S.A.

"I have received many opportunities here which would have never been possible for me in Russia," she said. "The liberal arts education at Columbia taught me not just a multiplicity of facts and equations but an understanding and appreciation of beauty in any form, be it a brilliant thought, an elegant experiment or an exquisite piece of music."

Elena, like most immigrants, came to America because it is a land full of opportunities. She admits that "because of the rampant anti-Semitism in my native land, had I stayed in Russia, as a Jewish woman I would have had very limited opportunities for either education or a professional career." However, in America those limitations do not exist. In September 1996, she continued the pursuit of her lifelong dream of becoming a doctor when she enrolled at Cornell University Medical School.

I believe that the vast majority of immigrants, particularly those who come by choice, are stars in the making. Something inside of them says, "We want more." A study of our solar system reveals that the brightness of a star comes not from the outside surface but from within, deep within. And so it is with immigrants. They have a burning desire deep within them that gives rise to their ability to shine.

A burning desire deep within motivates them to go beyond boundaries of land, sea, and self. Something deep inside moves them to come to America. They know that here in America, what was formerly impossible is now possible. They come because they recognize that America offers opportunities and rewards for honest endeavors.

Lata Krishnan, an Indian brought up in East Africa and England, was drawn to California's diverse environment of both high- and low-tech industries. Ms. Krishnan said, "America in general, and California in particular, is a very fertile ground with opportunities that you can take advantage of and make things happen. That is something that people have read about and seen in movies, and I do believe is true.

"Having experienced some discrimination as a nonwhite [in England], I found California very welcoming."

In 1988, Krishnan and two other Indian partners started Smart Modular Technology in Fremont. The firm is now one of Fortune 500's fastest-growing technology companies, employing over two thousand in California and overseas.

Yes, immigrants come because America is where hope lives, where ambition thrives, and where the impossible becomes possible.

As a nation of immigrants, it is the immigrant in all of us that has created the American dream. It is a part of us that many have forgotten and need to recall in order to make that American dream live again.

If you want to *Make It in America,* remember . . .

- America is where ambition meets possibilities.

- America is successful because it attracts ambitious people.

- America offers opportunities and rewards for honest endeavors.

In America anything and everything is possible.

Chapter 5

FREEDOM AND CHOICE

(WE CAN DO ANYTHING WE DARN WELL PLEASE)

Born free, as free as the wind blows, as free as the grass grows, born free to follow your heart.

–Born Free, © *Donald Black and Barry John, Screen Gems—EMI Music, Inc., 1966*

These are the words of a song that echoes in hearts of many.

Freedom! A feeling or state of being that transcends mere words yet is universally understood. Like an invisible magnetic force, it pierces deep inside one's soul and penetrates every fiber of one's being. So consuming is the desire for freedom that many are willing to risk life and limb to go to a place where it is said to exist.

Though millions of people have never experienced freedom, history shows they will fight to attain it, fight to protect it, and are even willing to die for it. A few years before the birth of America in 1762, the French philosopher Jean-Jacques Rousseau wrote, "Man was born free, and he is everywhere in chains." What he described then is still true today.

For many, freedom will not become a reality unless they leave their native homes and go to where freedom is cherished and preserved. That is why immigrants are drawn to America, "the land of the free and the home of the brave."

Immigrants understand that America is more than a refuge from dictatorship and oppression. America stands for freedom in all its forms—freedom of speech, of religion, of lifestyle. America is a place where man, woman, and child is free, not just physically but mentally. It is a place where minds are free to dream, create, and attain whatever one can conceive.

The corruption in many other countries makes it almost impossible to work or to live. Just to get a business license requires bribing many officials and overcoming many obstacles. That is why we read tales every day of illegal immigrants spending their last pesos to pay off the men who smuggle them into America. They would rather do that than work in dirty sweatshops and watch for the authorities, who could place them in jail or have them killed.

They are drawn by the fact that America both provides and encourages freedom. And it is in this wide-open freedom that immigrants find their entrepreneurial wings or an organization in which to nest and grow.

Surrounded by, and immersed in, freedom, immigrants become euphoric and push the limits. They devise frugal, practical ways to start businesses, expand, and create business opportunities. Their excitement and enthusiasm overflow, causing them to find creative, innovative approaches to defining and establishing themselves.

The urge for freedom is not only a key characteristic of the human spirit; it is also a major ingredient in fueling the desire and determination that leads to success. This yearning for freedom is alive not only in the heart and soul of immigrants, but is now resurfacing in the hearts of thousands of Americans. Every day, many leave stable, lucrative jobs and promising careers to pursue new avenues that offer more freedom.

Even large conglomerates are restructuring and selling off subsidiaries, many of which are now enjoying success as a result of their newfound freedom. An excellent example of this is Lucent Technologies. Since its spin-off from AT&T in 1996, it has been soaring like a hot Silicon Valley stock rather than a 123-year-old maker of phone equipment. From the time Lucent went public, its shares soared from 13½ to a high of 120 on January 8, 1999. According to *Information Technology* magazine, Lucent nearly tripled shareholders' money in 1998, compared with a 29 percent return for the S&P 500. Yes, large or small, freedom can be the fuel that launches both visions and dreams.

Jean-Jacques Rousseau's comment about man being "everywhere in chains" also applies to the invisible chains we place on our own ability to find freedom in our lives. Many of us are shackled by self-imposed limitations—"What will others think? What will my parents say? What if I fail?"

A good friend of mine is caught in the same dilemma I was in: whether or not to leave an unfulfilling job as a consultant for a failing software company. He is chained by illusions of success—the title, the corner office, the stock options. At this point, they are all of little value, but nonetheless, they are the hallmarks of the success he and society cling to.

He too has dreams of starting his own business, but hesitates. As he puts it, "Being president of a one-person business has no prestige."

He is afraid of what others will say. Let's face it, when people hear "consultant," some think "unemployed," "in-between-jobs," or "flunky." He is a part of the disillusioned majority—living in denial, deluding himself with illusions of success: the latest high-tech gadget and the suburban high-credit lifestyle. His ability to create and sustain a life with purpose and meaning is gradually slipping away. His decline is as certain as if he were chained to the gallows of a sinking ship, yet he is afraid to jump.

As of the writing of this book, he still hasn't left that failing company. And if the tide doesn't change within a year or two, he will certainly go down on that sinking ship. I firmly believe it is not misplaced loyalty, but rather fear, that holds him captive.

Freedom is a privilege and a choice. In America you are free to choose to dream, to do, and to become anything you want. You are also free to fail.

America holds out the promise that with hard work, anything and everything is possible. But if you are to receive the rewards of the free enterprise system, you must first be willing to free yourself and take the leap of faith. You must be willing to pay the price by exercising your freedom of choice.

If you want to *Make It in America*, remember . . .

- Fear can often hold us captive.

- It takes courage to break free from the chains that bind.

- America is a place where the mind is free to dream, create, and attain whatever it can conceive.

Freedom is a powerful inalienable right,
which yields rich rewards—
but only if we choose to exercise it.

Chapter 6

PRIDE AND PREJUDICE

(MELTING POT OR POT OF STEW)

I didn't know I was black until I came to America.

I arrived in New York on Saturday, March 30, 1968. Talk about excited! I was still flying high long after the plane touched down.

I had come to America to conquer a new frontier. Like all true pioneers, I had faith and confidence as strong as steel. Like those long, slender rods of steel used to build towering skyscrapers, my feet were solidly grounded, and I was never in doubt about the direction I was heading. It was straight up.

I was eager and young, and the world was mine. There was nothing I couldn't do and nothing I couldn't become. My faith and confidence both in America and in myself would get me where I wanted to go.

This is how immigrants look at America. They know it is going to be hard. And they know it is going to take time, work, sweat, and of course, money. But the intangibles rarely cross their minds. My intangible was the color of my skin. It never occurred to me that the color of my skin could be more important than my immigrant status.

Five days after I arrived in New York, the Reverend Martin Luther King Jr. was killed in Memphis. As I watched TV, my armor of steel began to corrode.

My American family, the Sherwoods, also sat in deathlike silence. My Aunt Maude's favorite newscaster, Walter Cronkite, was solemn. The news clip showed policemen and guards turning firehoses and dogs on people who looked like me.

These people had to have done something terrible; surely it couldn't be simply that *they weren't white*. Was this really what life in America was going to be like? Surely there was some mistake.

I looked at my Uncle Charles. His face was drawn and pale. My cousin Irma sat with her arm around my aunt staring at the television, both of them had damp clumps of tear-filled Kleenex in their hands.

I had never thought of myself as black, or any other color for that matter. I was simply Jamaican, like others were American, English, or French. I was also female and a five-foot-three dynamo. I didn't know what being "black" meant. Or rather, what "black" meant in America. Truthfully, I wasn't prepared for life in a land of paranoia and boxes.

In Jamaica, nearly everyone would have been regarded as "black." However, this was never a stigma nor a barrier. My mother was an attorney, as was her father. One of her older brothers was a judge, the other a surgeon. Our friends were in similar professions. Jamaica was culturally rich and economically diverse, but being rich or poor was not based on black or white. In fact, nothing was.

I quickly learned that in America, everything is neatly organized in boxes. There were boxes for everything. A box for the whites, but not all the whites. There were different boxes for the Irish, the Italians, and the Germans. But, even if people appeared white, but were Jewish or Puerto Rican, they were put not in the white boxes, but in the Jewish or Latino boxes. It was unbelievable how many sections of boxes there were! From Manhattan's Delancey Street to the Grand Concourse in the Bronx, from Coney Island to Long Island, they all had their boxes. There were even boxes within boxes.

I found life in America was not at all a melting pot, but rather a pot of stew. Yes, we were all in the same pot, but there were distinct and noticeable differences.

From this experience I learned:

- That being unable to see something doesn't mean it's not there.

- *What I see is more important than what others see.*

Let me explain. Intellectually, we know that there are a myriad of stars and galaxies constantly orbiting our planet, but in the light of day, you can't see them. In fact, it is only at night that we are conscious of the stars. But just because we can't see them in the day, doesn't mean they are not there.

The fact is the pigment of my skin is dark. And just because I wasn't conscious of it didn't mean it wasn't so. Whether you call it black, California-golden, or chocolate brown, it isn't white. But what difference should that make if in America, or anywhere else for that matter, I am classified or boxed as "black"?

The critical issue is that what I see is more important than what others see. The girl who came to America was bright, talented, and unstoppable. Even today, I see a strong, talented, ambitious woman who can *do* anything, and who can *become* anything. No boxes can limit my dreams, confine my possibilities, or contain my passion. And no boxes ever will, unless I let them.

Prejudice, in its many forms, exists not just in America, but also all over the world. But because of the freedom that is available in America, even with its boxes-within-boxes, we must seize every opportunity. We must take advantage of any and all freedoms and choices in defining who we are, no matter what we are.

Take Ling Chai, who grew up in China. To avoid imprisonment and pursue the freedom she longed for, she escaped, leaving family and friends behind.

When she came here, she found things were not as she thought they would be. In fact, she says, "just like in China, there were preconceived notions of what men are expected to do as opposed to what women are supposed to do, and they certainly were not paid equally for doing the same work." Still, she encourages us, "Until perceptions change, we need to make sure that we don't let the world define who we are. We need to define those things for ourselves."

Immigrants have found that the ability to see under, around, and over obstacles is at the root of all success. We are not naive enough to think we won't confront obstacles of every kind. But in "the light" of our dreams we don't see them. Our dreams are so intensely real, and burn so strongly, that we see only possibilities.

If we are to move ahead, we cannot allow ourselves to be chained by limitations, real or perceived. Hanging on to past injustices will only rob us of our future.

California State Assembly member Nao Takasugi, in a speech to the National Japanese-American Historical Society at the Presidio in San Francisco, referred to one of the most shameful documents in the history of America. Executive Order 9066, signed by President Franklin Roosevelt on February 19, 1942, called for the forced internment of 120,000 U.S. residents of Japanese ancestry (77,000 of whom were American citizens). Takasugi said, "America must never again fall prey to the temptation to count its citizens by color."

Like true patriotic immigrant Americans, he refuses to be bitter. "I find I am compelled to remember the best of times, not the worst," he said. He then reminded the audience "to focus not on the grave deprivation of rights which beat us all, but rather on the countless shining moments of virtue that emerged from the shadows of that dark hour." He offered a Japanese phrase as his motto—"*gambate*," meaning work hard, never give up.

Therein lies one of the many secrets of immigrants. Leave the past in the past; free yourself to focus on the future.

Immigrants often see better tomorrows where others see only the failures of the past. They tend to see beyond obstacles and prejudices. They have hope and see only the possibilities.

If you want to *Make It in America*, remember . . .

- What you see is more important than what others see.

- Until perceptions change, we need to make sure that we don't let the world define who we are.

- We need to see possibilities where others see obstacles, to see hope where others see despair.

Labels don't have to be limiting.

Chapter 7

THE AMERICAN DREAM
(PROMISE OR GUARANTEE?)

Orlando Hernandez, a star pitcher on the famed Cuban National Baseball team, fled Cuba illegally on a makeshift raft with seven other defectors. Days later, he was picked up on a deserted island in the Bahamas.

On that raft, most wondered whether they would ever make it to the United States. Hernandez wondered the same thing. But he also had something else on his mind. Baseball was his love, and to pitch in the major leagues was his American dream.

One year later, in October 1998, Hernandez took the mound for the New York Yankees in the second game of the World Series against the San Diego Padres. When the night ended, his Yankees were one game closer to the World Championship and Hernandez was living his dream. He was also doing something he had always wanted to do—follow in the footsteps of the big brother he admired so much, the 1997 World Series Champion Florida Marlins MVP winner and pitcher, Livan Hernandez.

The story of Orlando Hernandez, now known to fans as "El Duque," is heartwarming but not unique. Since the first explorers set foot on the North American continent and stayed to build a nation, immigrants have risked life and limb not only to chase, but also to live the American dream. And in the process, they have learned a lesson that many Americans seem to have forgotten.

*The American dream is a **promise**, not a **guarantee**.*

It's a promise that here in America, you are free to dream, do, and become anyone or anything you wish. In other countries you may dream but have limited opportunities to make it happen. Or you may dream, but it's the government that will decide what you can do and what you can become.

In America you can do anything; your future is up to you. America provides the environment; however, you must seize the opportunities, take the initiative, and make it happen. Immigrants to this country certainly want a better life, but they know it is not a guarantee. They come because they know that in America, it is at least a possibility. Because in America, dreams come true.

One of the earliest lessons we are taught as children is not to feed wild animals, because if we feed them, they will forget how to care for themselves. They will become dependent on us for food. Regrettably, what we are disciplined enough to do for animals, we are not prepared to do for our fellowman. Some have chosen to break the basic rules of responsibility and survival.

The act of giving can be a two-edged sword. Although giving, in and of itself is good, it can be very dangerous. Some people give out of genuine generosity, others out of guilt. Some give because it makes them feel good, some to elevate themselves to the status of benevolent benefactor. However, giving often operates from a position of strength and can disempower the recipients. When done repeatedly, it can rob recipients of their self-esteem and render them incapable of taking care of themselves.

Also, some people take because they need, some because it is available, and some because it is the lazy way out. Unfortunately, many people today have become totally dependent on entitlements for their survival.

The often-echoed words of President John Fitzgerald Kennedy's inauguration speech, "Ask not what your country can do for you, ask what you can do for your country," are elegantly profound. When you ask what your country can do for you, you disempower yourself and remove yourself from a position of strength. It makes you dependent and reduces your choices and your chances of success.

On the other hand, when you say, "What can I do for you?" you are in a position to give, you are in a position of power. If you have *talent* and *skills* to give, employers and decision makers seek you out. If you have *time and money* to give, countless organizations and associations will fight over you. When you are in a position to contribute, you are in a control position and you are in demand.

We need only look at the dismal failure of communism to see how removing the individuals responsibility for and stake in his or her personal success leads to a lack of motivation and, ultimately, to downfall. Malcolm Forbes, the late American publisher, said it best, "When you cease to dream, you cease to live."

Remember always that the American dream is not a guarantee, it's a promise. It's a promise that here in America, you are free to dream, do, and become anyone or anything you wish. America provides the environment, but you must seize the opportunities, take the initiative, and make it happen. Immigrants have learned that the best way to make it in America is to earn it!

In America you can do anything; your future is up to you.

If you want to *Make It in America*, remember . . .

- The American Dream is a **promise**, not a **guarantee**.

- When you cease to dream, you cease to live.

- Earn what you take.

"Ask NOT what your country can do for you,
ask what you can do for your country."
—John F. Kennedy

THE FOUNDATION

The principles and values
which form the foundation
on which we build success.

Chapter 8

FAMILY

(A GIFT LIKE NO OTHER)

There's no vocabulary
For love within family,
Love that's lived in
But not looked at,
Love within the light of which
All else is seen, the love with which
All other love finds speech.
This love is silent.
            —T. S. Eliot

Last June, I had a delightful conversation with a wonderful taxi driver named A.J. He came to this country from Iran.

During our conversation, I shared with him the fact that I was writing this book and asked, "What, if any, differences have you seen between immigrants and Americans since you came to live in America?" I will share two of the many insights I gained from this incredibly sensitive man.

He remarked that many of his American co-workers commented that they don't know how he does it. He explained that sure, things are difficult, but he still sends 50 percent of everything he makes to his father in Iran. He continued, "I owe my father everything. My father taught me everything. My father sent me to college. We speak on the telephone every week. Father never once asks me for money. He doesn't have to. He knows how he raised his son."

Continuing, he said that when co-workers recently asked him where he was going on vacation, he told them he was going home to spend it with his father. They couldn't believe that he'd spend four weeks just visiting family. He said, "I don't understand. Why not? We are family. Family is the most important thing and what I miss the most."

I left A.J.'s taxi a lot richer than I had been when I got in. He helped me recall and appreciate what it means to be part of a family. Family brings the responsibility, but also the benefit, of being a part of something bigger than yourself.

To put it in A.J.'s words, "I am here because, as the eldest, I have the responsibility to help care for my family. And it is easier here to make money. I have a college degree and used to work in a bank back home but it didn't pay much. Here in America you can make money. I don't plan to drive a taxi forever. I work extra shifts and save my money. One day I will have my own business. But first I must help my family."

Yes, family responsibility is a high priority for immigrants. Nothing shy of a strong sense of responsibility would give someone the discipline to send 50 percent of everything he earns to someone not living under his roof. Let's face it, many of us find it hard enough to put away 15 percent to 20 percent of our earnings in our own retirement funds, much less give it away to someone else.

Hearing the emotion and conviction in A.J.'s voice helped me renew my appreciation for the opportunities that this country has afforded all of us. No question about it, America is far from perfect, but when all is said and done, immigrants come because America offers a multitude of benefits that we can't find anywhere else. And high on the list is the ability to provide a better life for our families, both materially and, in many cases, spiritually.

Another difference that came to mind as I listened to A.J. was how we spend our time. The newspapers are filled with stories of how Americans are constantly trying to juggle too many things—from work and climbing the success ladder to family and social obligations. We give our children good schools, dance lessons, and Little League, but very little family time.

A.J. reminded me of the *cycle* that is family. The relationship and sense of responsibility he has towards his father first began with his father. As parents, we need to teach our children what's important. It starts with us. We must give them more than money and material things. We must give them those important life-lessons that take personal time.

Have you ever heard a statement that seemed quite clear at the time, but whose depth you didn't fully appreciate until much later? That happened to me just last year.

As I wrote earlier, I came to the United States approximately thirty years ago. And I became a citizen 18 years ago, when the political climate of Jamaica changed dramatically and it became apparent that I would never return there to live.

A few years ago, a friend from Jamaica came to visit me, and on leaving, said, "Marcia, you know a lot of tourists, when they leave Jamaica, say 'you have a beautiful island and I had a great time, but I couldn't live here because of all the poverty.' Well, I feel the same way. America is great. I enjoy myself every time I come, but I couldn't live here because of all the poverty."

Her words caught me by surprise. I had never equated America with poverty. However, after she elaborated, I realized she was right. She saw a poverty of culture, a poverty of values, a poverty of life. But it wasn't until last year that the full importance of her words resonated with me.

I went back to Jamaica for my aunt and uncle's 50th wedding anniversary. The anniversary party was on Saturday night and we all had a grand time, with cousins and friends that we hadn't seen in years and years. Many came from Canada, England, the U.S., and from different islands in between. Needless to say, we partied until the wee hours of the morning.

Even though everyone was tired the next day, nothing could stop the family ritual.

And it was on that occasion, in one clear lucid moment, I understood what my friend meant. Every Sunday after church services, the entire family would get together—children, grandchildren, cousins, and "adopted" family members. I watched as the younger ones played soccer against the older ones, children and grandchildren against parents and uncles. As I stood outside watching the game, I could hear laughter coming from inside, where some of the women were deep into "girl talk." I instantly felt a deep sense of loss. In a very real way, my life in America indeed seemed poor.

It is sad to see how few families make the time to play and eat together. The kids are dropped off at Little League, tennis or gymnastics. They learn to play and bond with others, but not their families. They often grab fast food or eat in front of the television, but seldom with other family members.

Mealtimes should be more than simply sharing food. Mealtimes are for sharing yourself. Even the business world appreciates the importance of "breaking bread" with others. Expense accounts abound and every attempt is made to bond with the prospect or the customer. What about our children? What about our families? Why can't we make the time, at least once a week, to break bread and bond with them?

Drive through any ethnic neighborhood on a Sunday and witness the large family gatherings, whether composed of Latinos, Italians, Asians, West Indians, or some other nationality. Many families bypass various career options and choose to live close to each other, because they value the importance of these family rituals. They chose to live in material poverty so as to be rich in life.

If you want to *Make It in America*, remember . . .

- Teach children the importance of family.

- Take time to bond as a family.

- Recognize that poverty comes in many forms.

The power of family can be as
strong as Steel.

Chapter 9

SELF-RELIANT

(GOD BLESS THE CHILD THAT HAS ITS OWN)

In 1826, fifty years after our Declaration of Independence, the English writer and essayist William Hazlitt observed, "the way to secure success is to be more anxious about obtaining it than about deserving it."

This is the mindset that our immigrant parents held when they first landed in America. However, a lot has changed over the past 200-plus years, particularly in the last 45. Many have forgotten that success must be earned. They have forgotten that all of us, Americans and immigrants alike, are responsible for our own success.

I believe many of my fellow Americans feel that not only do they deserve success, but that success is their birthright. Since America is successful, and we are Americans, we should be successful. There should be no prerequisites, no dues to pay, no questions asked.

So confident and assured are we of our right to success, that many automatically look to the government or their employers to make sure they have it. And they become angry, cynical, and even resentful if they don't get it.

Success, equality, and the pursuit of happiness are but illusions in many parts of the world. However, in America the probability of everyone achieving success is extremely high. And our Declaration of Independence supports us in our pursuit of it.

We hold these truths to be self-evident, that all men are created equal, that they are endowed by their Creator with certain unalienable Rights, that among these are Life, Liberty and the pursuit of Happiness.

However, with rights come responsibilities. And one such responsibility is to take care of oneself—to be self-reliant.

Once upon a time, Americans were self-reliant people. They were tradesmen, blacksmiths, and farmers. At the start of this century, over 85 percent of them were self-employed. But by 1960, things had changed dramatically. The numbers literally reversed themselves, with more than 85 percent of laborers working for other people or for the government. We had slowly shifted from being an independent society to being a dependent society.

By the 1960s, we belonged to big unions and even made sure to elect officials who would sponsor legislation that would take care of us. We had changed from a society that took total responsibility for ourselves to one that depended on other people or the government for our very means of earning a living. Then came the 1980s. It became our time of reckoning.

The business climate we knew changed dramatically between 1980 and 1990. We were riding the crest of one of the longest economic booms in U.S. history—deregulation, budget cuts, tax cuts, "junk bonds," and leveraged buyouts. This precipitated an avalanche of mergers and acquisitions.

Then the wave crashed. Of the Fortune 500 largest companies, 230 disappeared or changed hands—a whopping 46 percent. Giant firms such as Kohlber Kravis Roberts (KKR) grew even bigger by acquiring other giants: RJR Nabisco, Beatrice, Borden, Owens-Illinois, and Safeway. Some giants, such as Eastern Airlines, went belly-up, while others, such as IBM, struggled to survive.

These cataclysmic changes continued into the 1990s, where we saw some of the biggest mergers ever. We saw the biggest automobile merger—Daimler Benz and Chrysler ($40.4 billion); the biggest banking merger-Travelers Group and Citicorp ($72.5B); the biggest telecommunications merger—SBC Communications and Ameritech ($73.3B); and the biggest oil and gas merger—Exxon and Mobil ($86.3B). And the merger madness hasn't stopped. The biggest yet is still to come: the proposed Sprint/MCI/WorldCom merger for $115 billion.

Four of the ten largest deals involved banking, an industry that still carries heavy overcapacity, and three involved telecommunications. Many people who thought they had jobs for life are suddenly finding themselves in unemployment lines. Even today, many are witnessing their parents and friends being laid off, sold out, and turned out by corporations that once promised the world and even at one time called them "family."

Many Americans have witnessed firsthand the pain and sorrow that come from relinquishing control and trusting in the promises of others. And this is where we can learn from the immigrants who came before and who continue to come to this great land.

Whether the promises come from big business, big unions, or big government, immigrants know that you should never give someone else ultimate responsibility, and therefore control, over your future.

Phyllis Cano is a living testament to this. At one point she gave up control, but then took it back.

Nine years ago, Phyllis Cano was a single mother with little education living on welfare. Phyllis realized that as long as she was dependent on the government, she would have no future. So she obtained a loan from the Small Business Administration and attended entrepreneurial training at Mi

Casa Resource Center for Women in Denver. She then went out on her own and started her own business.

Phyllis received the Small Business Administration's Welfare-to-Work Business of the Year Award in 1997. And today, she is the owner and operator of two bakeries in Colorado specializing in custom-made cakes.

Remember, promises can be broken. If we want to have a future with any semblance of success and certainty, we must take responsibility for making it happen. We must become self-reliant.

If you want to *Make It in America*, remember . . .

- The way to secure success is to be more anxious about obtaining it than about deserving it.

- Never give anyone ultimate responsibility and control over your future.

- Take responsibility for making it happen.

> "Do not let what you cannot do
> interfere with what you *can do*."
> **—John Wooden**

Chapter 10

SACRIFICE WITH A PURPOSE

(HANG IN THERE)

Almost everyone living in America has come across one or more neighborhood convenience stores owned by an Indian immigrant. One such store is even a permanent feature on *The Simpsons* TV show.

Many of these highly qualified owners are doctors, engineers, professors, and lawyers from India. They slogged through several years of professional training to achieve careers that lent them status and earned them a comfortable living. Yet they tossed it aside to become shopkeepers.

The publication *India West* says, "Their accents may occasionally be the butt of American jokes, but it's the franchises who are laughing all the way to the bank.

"Buying a 7-Eleven store was the beginning of a mini-empire for new immigrant Ravi Grewal back in 1984. Equipped with a master's degree in food sciences, the Punjabi entrepreneur was set to embark on an academic career by pursuing a PhD. However, an uncle persuaded him to go into the convenience store business and he bought his first 7-Eleven store."

"I have never regretted the decision," Grewal told the India West publication. He now owns Subway sandwich shops, and Arco AM/PMs; he is in the process of franchising his auto registration and insurance businesses.

"My first store is the backbone of my success. It allowed me to expand; today I am flourishing," he added. His extended family owns nearly fifty 7-Eleven franchises.

You will travel many roads on your way to success, and one you will most certainly have to take is that of sacrifice, which comes in many forms. For some, sacrificing entails giving up the prestige and respect of a professional title and career. For others, it may be passing up current luxuries and pleasures in exchange for a bigger and better future.

This postponement of gratification is also becoming a trend in some nonimmigrant circles, as evidenced by an August 1999 article in *Fortune* magazine entitled "MBAs get .com fever."

"For MBAs at Harvard Business School, an offer from top consulting firms used to be as good as it gets: a six-figure starting salary, a $30,000 signing bonus, a pledge to pay for some or all of their B-school tuition—which amounts to more than $50,000." However, today's graduates are saying no to all that in favor of entrepreneurial and high-tech start-ups.

This new breed of Americans, like their immigrant counterparts, hunger for their "piece of the pie." They are crossing oceans, borders, and states. And like their forebears, they too are heading to the West Coast. They are heading straight for Silicon Valley.

The similarities between them and their immigrant peers can be readily seen. They are willing to take the risks, embrace the challenges, and accept responsibility for their own success.

These sacrificing and self-reliant mavericks are prepared to even buck the popular trend of immediate gratification by accepting lower-paying jobs in return for the long-term gains of stock options and the pursuit of the dream.

Immigrants have always looked ahead. They have always sacrificed now so that they and their children would have more *later*. With new, under-35 techno-millionaire role models to follow, these new pioneers readily leverage everything for the dream. Like their immigrant counterparts, they understand that there is a price to pay for success. They also understand that it will take time. So they work, and they wait.

Every entrepreneur and every new business owner truly interested in the future of his or her business draws much less in salary than he or she really earned. It is understood that this is a necessary price to pay to build a future.

All investors or business owners know that it is not how much you make now that matters, but how much you stand to make in the future that counts. And it's not how few customers or contacts you have now, it's how many you can have in six months or six years.

Even if you are not starting a business, but simply preparing for a lifestyle change, you must surely wrestle with similar things. Whether saving for college, buying a new house, or saving for retirement, learn from your immigrant roots. Prepare to live on less now, because your future is worth it. When the goals are worthy and noble, the means are of little consequence and the sacrifices are insignificant. *Prepare to live on less now, because your future is worth it.*

While reading *The Nudist on the Late Shift* (Random House, 1999, 248 pages), I found myself smiling as author Po Bronson described Sabeer Bhatia's apartment.

Sabeer Bhatia is the genius behind the incredibly successful HotMail Internet company. As Bo tells it,

> One night I met Sabeer for a glass of sweet Indian rum at his apartment in Bayside Village, south of Market. Bayside Village is a five-story, three-dimensional crossword puzzle of boxy apartments. His humble apartment has a bachelor pad decor with unadorned, white-spackled walls; a framed print leaned up against the living room wall, a rug was rolled up off to the side. It is the same apartment he had the night he wrote the HotMail busi-

ness plan. It's definitely not the place I expected from a man who's worth a couple of hundred million dollars.

No doubt Sabeer has moved on to bigger and better quarters by now. But his story highlights that for many immigrants, the display of wealth is neither a priority nor the driving force. Immigrant entrepreneurs like Sabeer, know the rewards will come in time. The first priority is the sowing of the seeds, not the harvesting of the crop.

The most compelling story of sacrificing with a purpose is the one I read in Gwen Kinkead's book, *From Chinatown: A Portrait of a Closed Society.*

> Many immigrants start out as street peddlers. In three or four years, they have saved enough—between $50,000 and $100,000—to start small businesses. I didn't see how that was possible until I met Mr. Lin. . . .

> Lin forgoes privacy and comfort not because he is poor, but to save money. He earns $360 a week peddling vegetables and fruit. Selling umbrellas is more lucrative, bringing in from $80 to $100 a day. His monthly income, Lin says with utter frankness, and with a relish common to most Chinese when they discuss money, averages $1,800. He has saved some $18,000 of his annual $22,000 income in each of the last four years . . . All . . . told, Lin has $70,000 tucked away for a small business.

> I asked Lin how it was possible for him to save eighty percent of his income.

> He explained that he spends only $250 a month—the money for his rent, a few dollars on the telephone, and about $100 on food. "Rice very cheap," he said, smiling. "And boss gives me lunch."

From time to time we all need reminders that sacrifice is a core characteristic of both successful people and successful businesses. Both immigrants and Americans must pay the price for success.

Sacrifice with a purpose is common in the immigrant community and delayed gratification is the norm. How long to delay that gratification is up to the individual.

This land abounds with opportunities for all, but it is we who must take advantage of them. Success is ours for the taking. It is not up to our parents, our teachers, or our managers to make us successful. We must take responsibility for our own success. It is we who must be prepared to pay the price and sacrifice. It is we who must sacrifice with a purpose.

As Shakespeare wisely penned in *Julius Caesar*, "the fault, dear Brutus, is not in our stars, but in ourselves . . ."

If you want to *Make It in America*, remember . . .

- Take the risks, embrace the challenges, and accept responsibility for your own success.

- Sacrifice with a purpose.

- Make sowing the seeds your first priority, not the harvesting of the crop.

Give up what you desire today
so you can live your dreams tomorrow.

Chapter 11

A DEBT IS OWED

(THE ROAD WAS PAVED)

We have come to glorify youth and dismiss the wisdom of our elders and the respect we owe them. We all need to be reminded of that huge debt; they paid the price and paved the way for us.

Today, many have come to have little regard for those who came before. In our "go-go-go" society, what happened five years ago is ancient history. We hear that the only thing people care about is WIIFM—what's in it for me?

It is not a coincidence that adult baby-boomers have been commonly referred to as "The Me Generation."

Immigrants came to America and worked so that future generations could have more than they did. They worked so that they could bring their families over from the old country. They worked so that their descendants would have a better life.

As the descendants of the great waves of immigrants from the start of this century become third- and fourth-generation Americans, this connection to those who came before can still be seen in some ethnic neighborhoods.

My friend Vincent shared with me an interesting story of one of the ways respect was taught in his neighborhood. He grew up in an old-fashioned Italian neighborhood, where things such as honor, respect, and family were valued. In this neighborhood of immigrants and children of immigrants, they felt a level of respect was due particularly to the elders who paved the way.

He remembers a kid named Joey, who was more of a punk than a pal. Joey never listened to anyone. He was a bully and a know-it-all. He would take advantage of everyone and everything.

One day, word got around that Joey had taken advantage of an elderly widow in the neighborhood. This was unacceptable.

In an Italian neighborhood certain things are sacred. The bond of loyalty and trust between ordinary people rivals that between a doctor and a patient. You know whatever is said in confidence will go no further. You also know that "certain things" are best taken care of in the community.

This was one of those things. So one night, a number of older guys "jumped" Joey. They blindfolded and tied him up. They dumped him in a neighborhood on the other side of the tracks, one where he was clearly not welcomed. What happened after that I will leave to your imagination. Needless to say, Joey learned his lesson. He learned that everything has a price.

Some children of immigrants never forget that someone else paid the price for what they enjoy today. They learned the lessons immigrants teach their children about respecting those who paid the price before:

- Don't take your forebears' efforts for granted.

- You owe a debt to those who made your life possible.

Immigrants have always been appreciative of those who came before. All immigrants know they owe a debt to the first of their kind who came to America and paved the way. They owe a debt to all those who formed support groups to help them during their relocation. These groups were there to assist with everything from finding housing and jobs to obtaining medical services and discount goods.

The literature of America's immigrant experience is filled with stories of the Italians, Irish, Jews, Chinese, Russians, Blacks, and others who endured the hardships, faced the prejudice, and stood their ground so that those who came later would not have to.

No matter who we are, immigrant or native-born American, we cannot forget those who came before. Either directly or indirectly, they have helped us get where we are today. As a woman of color in America, I owe a huge debt to such people as:

- Jane Adams, who from her Hull House in Chicago beckoned immigrants toward the American dream and crusaded for labor reform, universal suffrage, and other injustices against women and minorities;

- Rosa Parks, who refused to give up her seat to a white man on a bus in Montgomery, Alabama, and launched the civil rights movement;

- Betty Friedan, who was fired after requesting a second maternity leave, and helped to redefine feminism and ignite the women's movement;

- Dolores Huerta, who co-founded the United Farm Workers with Cesar Chavez in 1962 and is one of the 20th century's most powerful and respected labor movement leaders.

- Chien-Shiung Wu, the late pioneering physicist and Columbia University professor who radically altered modern physical theory and changed our accepted view of the structure of the universe. Wu became the first woman to receive the prestigious Research Corporation Award given only once every five years as well as the Comstock Prize from the National Academy;

- And many, many others on an endless list.

Black and minority musicians owe a debt to the likes of:

- Marian Anderson, the first black singer to perform with the Metropolitan Opera;

- Duke Ellington, who received the Pulitzer prize posthumously in 1999

- Tito Puente, who virtually invented the music called Salsa and influenced artists from Miles Davis to Carlos Santana;

- the one and only Louis Armstrong,

- As well as Paul Robeson, who belongs in a class by himself.

Black athletes owe a debt to Joe Louis, Jesse Owens, Jackie Robinson, and Arthur Ashe, to name a few.

These pioneers endured much and broke barriers so that we can enjoy the freedoms that we have today.

In February 1999 a football player for the Atlanta Falcons forgot he owed a debt and thought only of himself. His transgression was not the result of a moment of weakness but rather a deliberate, well-thought-out act of selfishness. The night before the Super Bowl, the biggest game of the season, he left his family and teammates and went alone to procure the services of a prostitute.

He left not one, but two families. He left his wife and child, and he left his team. This man did not make it all the way to the Super Bowl by himself. Over the years, many people put a lot of hard work into getting him to that place in time. He owed it to them to make good on their investment. He owed his parents, he owed his wife, he owed every member of his team, he owed his coaches, he owed the city of Atlanta, and he owed the fans.

No man is an island. We are part of a whole. We live in families, we live in communities. Every public official, every athlete, every entertainer has an obligation to the people who pay their salaries: the public.

Yes, we all have debts to pay—sometimes to those who paved the way, sometimes to those who pay our way.

If we are to be successful as individuals and as a people, we have to once again recognize that we have a responsibility—that no one becomes successful by themselves. As such, our fates are inextricably linked together.

No matter what the organization, whether business, nonprofit, or Little League, there is a price to pay for success. And that price is bigger than any one person can pay. Success lies in our comradeship and our commitment to our goals and to each other.

If you want to *Make It in America,* remember . . .

- No man is an island.

- Others paid the price and paved the way.

- A debt is owed to those who came before.

Respect those who broke down the barriers.

Chapter 12

KNOWLEDGE AND WISDOM
(THEY CAN'T TAKE THAT AWAY FROM YOU)

If a man empties his purse into his head no man can take it away from him. An investment in knowledge always pays the best interest.
  —Ben Franklin

There is an old Jewish tale in which three men are riding on a boat together. One is a wealthy manufacturer; the second, a successful salesman; and the third, a teacher.

The wealthy manufacturer is well-dressed, wearing the latest in fashion. His hands are adorned with rings, and he carries a diamond-studded walking stick. The salesman, talkative and self-promoting, makes his presence known everywhere he goes. The teacher, dressed in subdued, dark clothes, speaks softly and reads.

In a conversation, the wealthy manufacturer brags about the huge factory that sits in the coastal town that is their destination. He talks about how many tons of goods he produces in a year and how such a factory will assure him of the good life for many years to come.

The salesman brags about his beautiful home in the coastline city and about how much money he will make when the goods he is ferrying on the boat get to the port.

They deride the plain, homely teacher, who carries with him but one book. "If I were a teacher," they say, "I would own whole libraries." The teacher replies softly, "I do not need libraries. The information in this book remains in my head long after I read it."

The material-rich businessmen look upon the teacher with contempt.

Just before they arrive at their destination, a sudden, massive storm appears in the sky. Packing hurricane winds, it tosses the boat and dumps the three men and the salesman's goods into the sea. The storm reaches epic proportions as it hits land, destroying the factory and much more in its path.

Amazingly, the three men survive. However, the businessman has lost his factory and his business is ruined. The salesman's goods are gone—he will make no money from their sale—and his beautiful house is leveled. Torn and tattered, the two men wander the city. As they turn a corner, they see the teacher standing in the ruins with his class, teaching as if the school building had not collapsed.

The two men greet the teacher like long-lost family members and tell him their tale of woe. They remark at how the teacher looks none the worse for wear. The teacher reveals his secret.

"The manufacturer has his factory, his money, and his goods. But when they are gone, they are gone. The salesman makes lots of money and buys a beautiful house, but when it is gone, it is gone. But I have only the knowledge that fills this head. No storm can take it away. Nobody can steal it. And most importantly, I can give it away without losing it."

Immigrants are raised on stories like this one. Having lived in often indescribably poor conditions, they know the value of the simplest things. For many immigrants, education is the most important of the wonders that America offers.

The Jewish people have always been known as the "people of the book." And they have always held on to the idea that learning is sacred, and that knowledge makes a man or woman richer than any amount of money.

So when the great wave of Jewish immigrants came to this country, the first thing they did was to enroll their children in the public school. In New York City, millions of Jewish and other immigrant children took advantage of the then-free college education at such institutions as City College and Brooklyn College.

It was not a handout they sought. It was not a favor. They only asked for the opportunity to make their way. "Give us the opportunity," they said, "and we will do and learn the things we need to do to make it in America."

Immigrants have learned that you do what you need to do. There is not time to moan about past injustices and hard times. There is only now. And the more you know, the more you can be.

While I have told you the tales of those who came here and became greatly successful, most immigrants created a life for themselves here that will never be recorded in the annals of history, business, or technology. But their stories are examples of how immigrants used their knowledge and wisdom to live a full life.

Aron Verschleiser came to the U.S. as a young man, seeking a better life than the one he had in what was then Austria-Hungary. His first wife died, leaving him with two young children. He remarried and had four more. When the Great Depression hit, the oldest of his children was barely a teen. Tillie, his wife of 56 years, lost her sight as she approached middle-age. It was not an easy life.

Aron and Tillie opened a knitting store in Bensonhurst, Brooklyn. They sold wool and other items associated with knitting. Profit margins were thin, so family members pitched in for little or no salary. His daughter Henny (he later named the store "Henny's Knitting Shop") taught post-World War II mothers how to knit sweaters, slippers, and other items for their expanding baby-boomer families. She shared her knowledge so that others could learn.

One would not call Aron a "shrewd" businessman. But he was smart. Bensonhurst was not only an enclave of Jewish immigrants and immigrant children, but it was also home to a majority community of Italian immigrants and their children, as well as several other ethnic groups. Aron, who was brought up speaking Yiddish and read the Yiddish newspapers every morning, learned not only to speak English, but also Italian, German, and parts of several other languages.

Why? Because he knew that knowledge leads to success, and knowing how to speak Italian allowed him to serve his customers better.

Socrates said, "Prefer knowledge to wealth. One is transitory, the other perpetual." Millions of immigrants have learned that every experience brings knowledge and that tomorrow will be better because it brings more knowledge. And Aron Verschleiser saw many tomorrows in his 98 years.

To this point, Peter Drucker said, "We know a lot about what's past and no longer needed. The future may be different, it may look nothing like what you are accustomed to, but don't discount what you know. Knowledge is never wasted. It just needs new application."

One of the reasons immigrants can come to America and be so successful in a short period of time is that they bring with them the knowledge and wisdom of the past. Many were successful once before and so they know how to be so again.

Those who place their trust in money and material things often find that those can be taken or quickly lost. But those who put their faith in knowledge know that it can never be taken away from them. Moreover, the more they share their knowledge, the more they acquire themselves.

If you want to *Make It in America,* remember . . .

- Education is one of the most important gifts America has to offer.

- Knowledge makes you richer than money ever will.

- The more you share your knowledge, the richer you become.

- Use what you've learned and share what you know.

> "Knowledge is not simply another commodity.
> It is never used up. It increases by diffusion,
> grows by dispersion."
> **—Daniel Boorstin**

Chapter 13

COMMUNITY

(UNITED WE STAND, DIVIDED WE FALL)

Today's materialistic society often defines stature and status by the amount of possessions and wealth you have. The more you have, the more power you have, the more respect you get. From the boardroom to the prison yards, respect and power is everything. As the saying goes, "It is better to reign in hell, than serve in heaven."

The sad truth is that immigrants usually arrive in America with few or no possessions. As a result they are often regarded as persons of little value, and therefore given little respect or consideration.

However, many immigrants working at menial jobs once held lucrative careers and lived pampered lifestyles in their former homelands. Many were doctors, lawyers, or professionals of some sort, but now find themselves accepting work and living conditions worse than any they had back home.

Psychologists have found that there are two things most humans need and are looking for:

- Feelings of belonging, and

- Feeling good about oneself and having others share those feelings.

This is where the community comes in. Immigrants usually get respect within their communities. People recognize and remember them and give them the respect they deserve and need. At the end of the day, or the end of the week, they return home to be fortified. In order to endure another grueling day or week, they return to where their souls are fed. They return to respect and dignity. This is one of the main benefits of communities and ethnic neighborhoods.

Outside of their communities, immigrants are often talked about, even in their presence, as if they weren't there. They are ignored and discounted, not just mentally, but physically. It is not uncommon for them to overhear their co-workers making disparaging remarks about them, their people, or their customs, rarely with apology.

In their communities, they have a sense of belonging. Life is less stressful, because the customs, food, and music are all familiar. They are not judged by what they do for a living. Many are given the respect they had back in their homeland because people know them, or they know of them. They are respected not for material possessions, but by enduring qualities such as honor, integrity, and sense of family.

Many a displaced American I know would welcome similar courtesies. When you no longer have the corner office or the big corporate title, the identity crisis begins.

Without love and support we would wither and die. This sense of community goes back to the dawn of civilized man. In ancient Greece they tell the tale of how the famed Helen of Troy suffered greatly when she was separated from her people. She not only lost all sense of who she was, but she almost lost her mind.

Legend has it that after one of many battles, her Greek soldiers returned home by ship to discover that the beautiful Helen was missing. Her husband, Menelaus, at great danger to himself, returned to the battle area to search for her. He eventually found her at a seaport village. She was suffering from amnesia. With her identity and self-esteem gone, she had become a nobody. She had sunk to the lowest level possible. She had become a prostitute.

Despite Helen's poverty and dirty appearance, Menelaus could not miss her inescapable beauty. Recognizing her, he called out her name. "Helen!" he shouted. Instinctively, she immediately turned around. As he informed her of who she was, her back straightened and her regal demeanor returned.

She was a nobody until someone remembered who she was. She was a nobody until somebody gave her back what she had lost: her identity and respect.

Immigrants, from the time they come to America, create communities that serve as "safe areas" for them, their families, and those immigrants who come later. We all need communities in our lives, both at home and at work.

Just think of how willing and able you are to work in a company or department that values you. Think of the best jobs you've had and ask yourself what it was that made that company so good to work for. Chances are that you felt some kind of a camaraderie or community within your area or within the company.

Like immigrants, we can create environments in our lives that make us feel safe but also allow others to enter and feel safe themselves. The immigrant, as we've said before, remembers that he owes a debt to those who came before and must help those who come after. That is community.

It is something we all need.

If you want to *Make It in America*, remember . . .

- We all have the need to feel good about ourselves and to have others share those feelings.

- It is impossible to "make it" without a sense of identity and respect.

- Communities nurture our souls and fortify our spirit.

Surround yourself with people who believe in you and accept you for who you are and can help you believe in YOU.

Chapter 14

DESIRE AND DETERMINATION

(YOU'VE GOT TO WANT IT, AND WANT IT *BAD*)

When I tell people I left Jamaica to make a new life in America with less than $500 in my pocket, I often hear the same thing:

"I wish I had your courage."

The truth is, I've never given much thought to courage.

Courage is not something I think about. Actually, if I stopped to think about how much courage it would take, I probably wouldn't do half of the things I do. Isn't that true for you too? If we thought about it, chances are we wouldn't strap our legs to two thin, slippery strips of wood and go sliding down a narrow tree-lined path covered with snow. If we thought about it, we would call this insanity. Yet skiers do it all the time and call it fun.

If you think about it, it would be insane to leave a perfectly good boat and dive into the sea just to look at fish, eyeball-to-eyeball, 80 to 100 feet below the surface. Let's face it, *Jaws* or no *Jaws*, the fish has the advantage. Yet scuba divers make that plunge without ever giving courage a second thought.

What's needed is not courage, but a burning desire for the result or the experience. And if the desire is sufficiently strong, you will ignore logic, defy the odds, and go for it. Immigrants to America have been doing this for hundreds of years.

Did they have courage? Of course they had courage. Some may argue that without courage, they would not have been able to defy the odds. They simply would have quit; the fear would have been overwhelming.

That is true, to a degree. Mark Twain said, "Courage is *resistance* to fear, *mastery* of fear—not *absence* of fear. Except a creature is part coward, it is not a compliment to say it is brave."

No, courage is not the overriding characteristic in *Making It in America*. All the courage in the world will not give you the burning desire and the confidence in the final result that you need to succeed. It is not education, family connections, or money. These things are important, but not the deciding factors.

Truth be known, I came to live with cousins, and access to cash was only a phone call away. So courage, or having only $500, wasn't the issue.

However, most of the immigrants who have arrived in America during the past 300-plus years came without money, family connections, and often education.

Intelligence? I know many intelligent people, some whom I would even consider courageous. Yet they are not generally considered successful.

None of these characteristics are key indicators of success. I am convinced that there are only two real indicators of success—**desire and determination**.

Let me tell you my cousin's story. The island of Jamaica was once an island paradise. But gradually political corruption made it less than paradisiacal. The government had implemented very tight foreign currency controls which could result in the seizure of personal assets. Islanders who had acquired a comfortable way of life saw it quickly disappearing.

The government passed a ridiculous law limiting the amount of cash that could be taken out of the country to $100 Jamaican.

The conversion rate at that time was $1 Jamaican for 45 to 50 cents U.S. And in order to get U.S. dollars, you had to present your passport at the bank where they documented how much you were exchanging. This forced many to buy U.S. dollars on the black market at ridiculous rates. At the banks, $20 Jamaican would normally get you $9 U.S., but on the black market, it only netted you $1 U.S. All this was transacted with a great deal of secrecy, since the fine for being found with illegal dollars was a mandatory prison sentence. So purchases were made cautiously and never in very large quantities.

The price many often have to pay for freedom is extremely high. Most think about it long and hard. It is difficult enough picking up and moving across town, much less to a different country. All the odds must be weighed. All the risks must be evaluated.

Then the big day comes, the day that you determine it is too risky to keep that much cash on hand and that it is time to move the money to America. One had to be extremely careful, because informants were everywhere. It was not unusual for one member of a family to turn in another member of the family to the authorities.

My cousin got ready to transport his entire life savings, plus some funds for a close friend. The money was rolled neatly and secured with rubber bands and placed in a blue Pan Am carry-on bag.

He arrived at the airport. At the counter, the airline agent asked if he had any bags to check. In that split second he pondered the random searches that took place as one entered the boarding area, and said, "Yes." The woman put a claim ticket on the bag and stapled the other half to his ticket jacket. He held his breath as he watched her throw the bag, zipped but unlocked, onto the conveyer belt.

My cousin immediately walked into the rest room. In a stall, he removed the claim ticket, tore it into pieces, and flushed it away.

Random searches were done not just of carry-on bags but also checked bags. He did not want a prison term, which would certainly have been the case if the bag could be linked to him. It was one thing to lose everything you have worked for, but another thing to rot in prison for the rest of your life.

The flight from Kingston, Jamaica, to Miami, Florida, is only one-and-a-half hours, but for my cousin, it seemed like a lifetime. Times like these test your stress fabric. It's also at times like these you pray like you have never prayed before.

As he stood at the carousel in baggage claim, not knowing wether he would ever see that Pan Am bag again, all he could do was wait and pray. The bag finally came shooting down the beltway; he grabbed it, said thanks to God, and walked toward customs. He handed over his paperwork and asked to be taken away so as not to be searched in front of an airport full of prying eyes. He knew America opens its doors to many—in particular well educated and financially self-sufficient business men. With everything declared his belongings and papers verified and signed, he was now "legal" in the United States. He was ready to head to a U.S. bank to start his life anew.

Immigrants have learned that the sacrifices might be great and the risks enormous, but when desire and determination are combined, they produce a force of awesome proportions. They produce what is called the drive to succeed.

If you want to *Make It in America*, remember . . .

- Weigh the odds, evaluate the risks.

- Courage is mastery of fear, not absence of fear.

- The two real indicators of success are desire and determination.

You've got to want it, and want it bad!

Chapter 15

INGRAINED BELIEFS

(DEFY THE ODDS)

"Yes, I CAN!"

I've heard many versions of the following story, but this one is my favorite. It is short and sweet, but packs a powerful punch.

A group of frogs was traveling along when two of them fell into a deep vat of milk. All the other frogs gathered around the top. When they saw how deep it was, they resigned themselves to the fact that their two friends were as good as dead.

The two frogs tried with all of their might to jump out. But alas, it was too high. The other frogs kept shouting down to them, "It's impossible! No frog can jump that high." Finally, one of the frogs took heed and with his tired legs barely moving, he gave up and drowned.

The other frog continued to kick and jump as hard as he could. His friends once again yelled down to him that it was useless. But he just continued to jump, harder and harder. In time the milk began to curdle and thicken. Before long it was almost like butter, solid enough to lend a firm footing to his escape.

When he got out, the other frogs asked, "Did you not hear us?" The frog explained that he couldn't hear them clearly but was grateful that they all stayed and cheered him on. He added that he was inspired to try even harder because he didn't want to disappoint them. As they embraced, his friends didn't have the heart to tell him the truth.

This story teaches us three lessons:

- The spoken word can have enormous power.

- Words have the power to destroy or give life.

- When you are encouraged and inspired, you can do the impossible.

The critical element is how strong your belief systems are. We've all heard the stories of immigrants who come to America expecting the streets to be paved with gold. My favorite is an Italian version that goes like this.

"Well, I came to America because I heard the streets were paved with gold. When I got here I found out three things:

First, the streets weren't paved with gold; second, they weren't paved at all; and third, I was expected to pave them."

"Streets of gold" is just a metaphor for these eternal optimists. Immigrants hold the belief not that things CAN be better, but that things WILL be better. Strong beliefs are our only defense against negative, demeaning, and destructive words.

An encouraging word said to someone who is down can often lift her up and help her make it through the day. Likewise, a destructive word said to someone who is down can be all it takes to kill his desire to go on.

Yes, words are powerful. They can be the wind that fans the flames of our beliefs. Those mental pegs inside of us can be inspired and motivated by a kind act or an encouraging word.

These mental pegs are laid early in life and they are laid by words. Unfortunately, before they can even get a sense of who they really are, many people get gunned down with piercing, destructive words. They are never encouraged to aspire to reach great heights or to become a person of substance.

Even some well-meaning friends have been known to rob us of our dreams with powerfully poisonous words.

"Who do you think you are? You can't do that!" "You'll never make it."

"I told you it wouldn't work."

"Aren't we *good enough* for you anymore?

"Save yourself the heartache and expense, quit now."

Because of comments like these, many dreams and lives have been destroyed before they've even begun.

Adopt the immigrant mentality. Believe that the streets in America are paved with gold. Believe that life will be better. Believe that in America, anything and everything is possible. Believe that you can go anywhere, do anything, and become anyone you want. Because when you truly believe, you'll defy the odds.

This power, the power of beliefs, is not the exclusive property of immigrants. It is open and available to anyone, anywhere. In any state, in any city, no matter who you are, if you believe you can, you will.

Let me tell you about one woman who defied the odds and taught me the power of beliefs. She is Una Sanguinetti-Steele, a most remarkable person.

One sunny afternoon I was sitting in a car parked outside the main courthouse in Kingston, Jamaica. All of a sudden, soldiers with bayonets started emerging from the building, the sound of their heavy boots hammering on the hot pavement. Immediately behind them were four bound men. They were handcuffed and chained to each other, both at their hands and at their feet. My heart pounded as they shuffled closer. Then I noticed that immediately behind them was another row of soldiers with bayonets pointed at a 45-degree angle at the prisoners' heads. With heart pounding, mind racing, I stammered, barely getting out the words, "Who . . . Who are they? What . . . What did they do?"

Vin, the man driving my car, replied, "They are on trial for treason." (Many years later I found out it was the first case of treason ever tried on the island of Jamaica.)

No sooner had the prisoners passed than another commotion started. The crowd rushed up the steps of the courthouse as its doors opened.

By this time I was literally standing in the car, stretching my whole body out the window trying to see what was going on. I could hardly believe my eyes. The person they were all trying to speak with was Una Sanguinetti-Steele, my mother!

Like many women, she found herself having to raise children on her own—in her case, *four* children. She had lived a very privileged life and wanted no less for her children. So after leaving my father, she worked days, studied nights, and was admitted to practice law on August 13, 1952.

There weren't many professional women in Jamaica, or almost anyplace else, in 1952. There certainly were very few women attorneys, especially in the islands. This woman defied the odds. She gained a reputation for being one of Jamaica's sharpest criminal attorneys. It was for this reason that she was chosen to represent those four men.

She taught me that there are no obstacles if the desire for success is strong enough. She taught me that success at any time, in any land, calls for faith in God and faith in yourself. And that armed with those faiths and beliefs, you can defy the odds. I have come to truly appreciate the universal truth of this principle.

The great violinist Paganini is a stunning example of this. At one of his performances, one of his violin strings snapped. The audience gasped, but the virtuoso continued without missing a beat. He was playing beautifully on three strings, when suddenly another string broke. The audience once again gasped. Surely he couldn't continue with only two strings! But continue he did.

Then the unimaginable happened. A third string broke. For a brief moment, the virtuoso stopped. Raising his famous Stradivarius violin high in the air, he exclaimed, "One string and Paganini!" With matchless skill and discipline, this gifted violinist finished the selection on one string.

So ingrained and strong were his beliefs, that with unabashed defiance and panache, he defied the odds.

Simply put, *he believed.*

One of the greatest gifts we can give the next generation of Americans is the gift of belief in self, which spawns self-respect and confidence. Without these it is impossible to achieve any lasting success. This is the gift Jhoon Rhee is passing on.

Grandmaster Jhoon Rhee, a 10th Degree Black Belt, is considered the father of American Tae Kwon Do. In 1957, he left Korea with $46 in his pocket and enrolled at Southwest Texas State Teachers College in San Marcos, Texas. English was his biggest obstacle. It took him half an hour to read a single page.

Through perseverance and discipline, Grandmaster Rhee has become tremendously successful and has received a great deal of recognition for his achievements in Tae Kwon Do. However, what he is most proud of is the work being done in his schools and by his foundation.

Grandmaster Rhee knows that physical success, without mental and spiritual success, is meaningless. He knows the role beliefs and discipline play in achieving success. Therefore, his schools teach not only the physical techniques of Tae Kwon Do, but the inseparable mental aspects as well. He teaches others how to build true confidence and achieve success, with knowledge in the mind, honesty in the heart, and strength in the body.

His Joy of Discipline program helps inner-city kids by teaching them self-respect, self-discipline, and self-motivation. For this, former President George Bush named him and his foundation the 721st Point of Light.

If you want to *Make It in America*, remember . . .

- The spoken word is enormously powerful.

- Believe not that things *can* be better but that they *will* be better.

- When you truly believe, anything and everything is possible.

> The two most powerful words you will ever hear are
> **"I CAN."**

Chapter 16

A HIGHER SOURCE

(IN GOD WE TRUST)

Faith speaks when hope dissembles:
Faith lives when hope dies dead.
—*Algernon Charles Swinburne*

Faith of our fathers paved the way. Faith in God, and the desire to please Him, formed the foundation of what we call America.

The Puritans, the Pilgrims, Roger Williams in Rhode Island, William Penn and the Quakers, and so many other early settlers to America came seeking the right to worship as they wished, when they wished, and to whom they wished. Historians say that among those on the Niña, the Pinta, and the Santa Maria were Jews fleeing the Spanish Inquisition by traveling with Columbus.

From the very beginning, many Americans have believed there is no more important relationship in life than the one that exists between them and their God. It is the relationship that shapes all others in their life. That single relationship affects whom they marry, how they raise their children, how they conduct business, how they live their lives.

So precious, so personal, and so profound is that relationship that they would willingly go through imprisonment or torture than denounce their God. They believe that they owe their life and everything they have to their God. And they believe that with His help they can do anything, win battles, be cured of any sicknesses, conquer any evil, without His help they can do nothing.

That was how the very first immigrant Americans felt, and it is still how many feel today. Change the names and the faces; the history and plight of these very first Pilgrims have a lot in common with many a modern-day immigrant seeking religious freedom.

The Pilgrim story is taught to American children no matter what kind of school they attend—public, private, or religious. It is a tale of the strength of the immigrant conviction and the extent to which they will go to worship their God.

The English church separated from the Roman Catholic Church in 1534, after the pope refused to grant the request of King Henry VIII to have his first marriage dissolved. Soon after, the English Parliament officially recognized Henry as the "Supreme Head on earth, immediately under God, of the Church of England."

Nevertheless, there were smaller Protestant groups that did not agree with the now prevailing Anglican Church of England. Many of these came to be called Puritans because they wished to purify the Anglican Church of any vestige of Roman Catholicism.

Henry's daughter, after becoming Queen Elizabeth I, feared that she would lose her grip on the people if the Puritans were not held in check. She therefore introduced severe legislation against them. In spite of this, the various Puritan groups continued to meet secretly in private homes.

Under increasing pressure, this small group decided to flee to the Netherlands, at the time the only place in Europe where their opinions and practices would be tolerated. Emigration, however, was illegal. As secretly as possible, therefore, they sold their homes and everything else they could not take along, and in 1608 they went to Amsterdam by ship. It was in the Netherlands that the separatists began to think of themselves as pilgrims.

Gradually, more fugitives arrived from England, and the group grew. In time the Pilgrims began to feel unsettled. They feared that if the Spanish Inquisition spread to the Netherlands, they would be worse off than they were under King James. What should they do? They contemplated another very big move— this time to America.

On September 6, 1620, in a little 90-foot ship named the *Mayflower*, 24 families—a total of 102 passengers and a crew of 25—set sail from Plymouth, England, heading for America.

That is the saga of the first immigrant Americans. It took faith and courage for them to attempt an ocean voyage of 3,000 miles. Like many who followed, they came in a ship that was badly overcrowded and ill-equipped to contend with the dangerous North Atlantic waters. Was the price worth it? After nine long weeks on the ocean, the joy that exploded on deck when they sighted land said "YES!"

This is the shared experience of many who have entered this land in search of every kind of freedom. In America you are free to worship whom you want, when you want, where you want and how you want. You are even free not to worship at all, if that is your preference.

Religion has always been a vital part of most immigrants' lives. That is why at the center of most immigrant communities you will see the Church, the Kingdom Hall, the Mosque, the Shrine, the Synagogue, the Temple. These are the spiritual outposts for preserving their religious traditions. These outposts are also at the center of all sorts of social and cultural activities.

In fact, for many there can be no separation of personal life from their spiritual life. Their faith is their life. So compelling is their belief that many would rather die with their faith intact than live without it. Stripped of everything they hold dear, including sometimes their very family, immigrants take comfort in knowing the one thing that can never be taken away from them is their faith.

Yes, they believe in themselves and in America. But their main source of strength, comes from their faith in a higher source. And key to their ability to make it in America is that in America, they can freely praise and honor their God.

When looking for the answer to how immigrants continually find the faith and strength to go on in the face of overwhelming odds, we need only look to the faith they have in the God they worship.

If you want to *Make It in America,* remember . . .

- Freedom of religion is an American treasure.

- With belief in God, anything is possible.

- There is no more important relationship in life than the one you have with your God.

> With faith the size of a mustard seed, you can move mountains.

THE
FRAMEWORK

The cornerstones we use
to achieve our dream of
making it in America.

Chapter 17

MINDSET OF A WINNER
(THE WILL TO EXCEL)

Sometimes life throws us a curve and we find ourselves in a place not of our choosing. This can be either positive or negative, depending on our mindset.

Take for example, the difference in mindset between immigrants who came to America of their own free will and those who came against their will (slaves). Although both may have landed with only the clothes on their backs, it was their mindset that determined their ultimate fate.

Thankfully slavery has been abolished. So today if you find yourself in a place not to your liking, you don't have to stay there. Today you are free to go wherever you want. You can choose to emigrate—from poverty, from the ghetto, from all kinds of entitlements (government or corporate), from dead-end careers or places.

The same opportunities that America offers to immigrants are open to all Americans. However, it is up to us to take the initiative to seize them.

I believe most people have an internal compass that keeps them pointed in the right direction, often causing them to become uneasy when they are off course. The kind of restlessness immigrants feel is akin to what many of us have felt in our jobs, our organizations, and our lives. Yet only a handful take action and emigrate to new places in their lives. Many, out of complacency and fear, simply stay put.

Complacency and fear stop people from moving forward for many reasons; these may simply be a function of chronological age. Mid-life and mid-career are therefore excellent times to re-examine and take stock.

To jump past this complacency and fear, we must take a leap of faith that things can change, we can change, and our lives can get better. Remember that when you commit yourself to take this leap of faith, you are actually freeing yourself. You subconsciously give yourself permission to fail. And from that very moment you begin to see things differently.

You begin to view every failure as yet another growth opportunity. You also begin to react to failure differently. You no longer let failures get you down, but rather view them as experiences from which to move forward to a place where you never could have landed, had you not taken that initial leap.

Remember also that success, like beauty, is in the eyes of the beholder. Success to me is reaping the rewards of your labor, and feeling good about where and how that labor was invested. And success doesn't necessarily mean "financial gain." In fact, many pass on that, preferring instead to go for "heart gain."

The Patels of California went for both.

According to the *ABJ Business Journal*, "they immigrated to the United States from India in 1990. Their first jobs in America were at two fast-food restaurants—McDonald's and Sonic in Springfield, Illinois. It was very different from the life they left behind.

"In India, the Patels participated in a youth congress. Dipak Patel is a past president of the congress as well as a banker. Sangita, his wife, was an elected member of the municipal council and a sociology professor.

According to Dipak, they were eventually able to buy a not-so-late-model Plymouth for $1,800, and with $60 in gas, they headed west. Stopping at Ponca City, Oklahoma, the couple saw newspaper advertisements about jobs at IBP in Amarillo that came with good pay, medical benefits and other enticements.

Describing their first home, Dipak says, "No cooling system, no heating system. It was just like a small garage. But we were very happy."

The Patels have come a long way in achieving success. The Patels now own property on California's famous Route 66, are partners in a Holiday Inn Express, and, in partnership with others, are building a $2.4 million Microtel Inn & Suites in Albuquerque.

"Here is a lot of opportunity. Here is a lot of cooperation. Unbelievable," Dipak says. "We set goals. I have some dreams."

But the Patels have not stopped at making a good living and good investments. Because this land has been so good to them, they have decided to be good to the land. Together with other business owners in the area, they organized the Route 66 and Business I-40 Association in California. Each member business contributes funds that the organization uses to make improvements along the thoroughfare. Dipak is excited about the idea that soon, more trees will be planted along the roads.

"We have very small (landscaping) places here," Sangita said, "but we put five or six trees there—flowers, everything.

"Our goal is helping people—any kind of people. Through helping people, God helps us," Dipak said, describing the good fortune he and his family have found in America.

As mentioned in chapter 1, for most people success means both financial gain and heart gain. And from that perspective it would appear as if the Patels have achieved both.

Let me also say that there are many stories of unsung heroes who have sacrificed financial gain to achieve heart gain. And I debated long and hard as to whether they should also be included in this book. However, I have opted not to include them for two reasons. One, it would be extremely difficult to do justice to both without doubling the size of the book. Two, most people who buy a book about making it in America, would be buying mainly for the financial gain aspect. Therefore the majority of stories deal more with that aspect than with heart gain, although many include both.

I encourage you, as you go through the following chapters in the remaining third of the book, to reflect on how immigrants go after the financial gain and heart gain. Look at how they assess opportunities, scope out new territories, evaluate risks, and break free from the past. It can be insightful and helpful as you assess your future dreams and opportunities.

If you want to *Make It in America*, remember . . .

- Just because you find yourself in a difficult place doesn't mean you have to stay there.

- Opportunities abound. We must train ourselves to see them.

- Real success is always more about heart gain than financial gain.

> You've got to give back to the community—
> success is a continual give-and-take
> and giving back again.

Chapter 18

IMAGINATION AND GUTS
(BEST BUDDIES)

"The U.S. will find it hard to compete . . ." Those chilling words came from a most reliable source, the U.S. Council on Competitiveness. On behalf of a 150-member group of U.S. business executives, academics, and labor organizers, a 10-year strategic assessment of the U.S. economy was conducted. The findings were published in a report entitled "Competitiveness Index 1996."

When I came across the report, I couldn't believe my eyes. Surely they had made a mistake! The America I knew was economically competitive, outperforming all other advanced or developing countries. Yet they claimed America was losing ground to emerging courtiers like China, Korea, and India.

The more I thought about it, after weighing all the variables, the only thing I could come up with that those countries had that we seemed to be missing: hunger. Not the lack of food, but the willingness and drive to do whatever needed to be done to get to where they wanted to go. We had become comfortably complacent and they were still hungry.

I was forced to acknowledge that we were becoming lazy. Well, maybe not lazy from the perspective of sitting around doing nothing. The U.S. Gross Domestic Product (GDP) confirms that U.S. workers are extremely productive. But we have taken our leadership status for granted, and that's dangerous. Just ask IBM; they will tell you just how dangerous that can be.

As a whole, we are certainly less hungry than those developing countries. And studies show it often takes more work to maintain a first-place position than it takes to get into the first-place position.

The U.S. Council on Competitiveness warned that the U.S. would not be able to maintain its competitive edge simply by producing well-established, standard products more efficiently. Rather, it said, *U.S. business will have to be increasingly innovative in developing and producing products and services that other nations cannot produce.*

So creativity, innovation, and imagination are crucial factors in our long-term success. And if you want to find those qualities, take a look in our immigrant communities.

Creativity, innovation, and imagination were exactly the qualities that immigrants brought to the table during the last three centuries, enabling America to achieve the leadership position it enjoys. Unfortunately today, these qualities are often articulated but seldom fostered in the majority of American companies and organizations. Additionally, creativity and innovation will exist and grow only in secure environments, places where people feel secure, places where they have the ability to try, to make mistakes, and to fail without fear of losing their jobs, their funding, or their projects.

This is where some immigrants have an advantage. Whether entrepreneur or intrapreneur (free agent within an organization), the one thing they have is the ability to see what others don't see. And one reason they are able to do this is because they're not afraid of putting everything on the line.

One such intrapreneur with imagination and guts that I greatly admired was the late Roberto Goizueta, CEO of the Coca-Cola Company.

Goizueta fled Castro's communist Cuba in 1961, leaving behind an affluent life of luxury to pursue freedom. He brought with him his family, a suitcase, and 100 shares of Coca-Cola stock. He believed that in the U.S.A. he could start over, and that all things are possible in the U.S.A. This was a man of vision, courage, and action who believed in his company and his abilities. Roberto Goizueta made a difference everywhere he went.

When he became CEO in 1981, he displayed vision, courage, and leadership when he "colored outside the lines" by introducing Diet Coke and by extending the company's trademark to products other than Coca-Cola. During his 16 years at the helm, Coke's market value grew from $4 billion to $150 billion. As a visionary leader, he helped thousands of others to realize their dreams. He would encourage and inspire them to go beyond the accepted.

Once he was asked where he got the courage to undertake some of his more unconventional visions. Drawing on his immigrant experience, he said, "Once you lose everything, what's the worst that can happen to you?"

Goizueta's example shows us that in business, as in life, success calls for a combination of creativity and guts, the same combination that millions of immigrants have used to find ways to leave their countries and come here. The imagination they used in overcoming the risks of leaving such places as communist East Germany, Vietnam, and other places is legendary.

Yes, imagination and risk are closely linked. But many executives today are too scared to take those risks. They seem more interested in growth through acquisition than growth through innovation and service. They are more interested in how the market is doing than how their customers and employees are doing.

Executives and their companies need to care enough to anticipate customer and employee needs, to care enough to make the workplace and the buying experience stress-free and more enjoyable.

I believe that is one of the reasons so many skilled employees are breaking free of corporate restraints today. Like immigrants of the past, they are becoming external free agents by the droves. These Americans are hungry to find not just a *cheaper, faster* way, but they are hungry to find a *better* way. They are hungry for a better life; they are hungry for compassion and truth; they are hungry for meaningful change.

That is why, like their immigrant friends, they leave in search of fertile ground and are willing to go wherever it exists. They are not deterred by risks and hardships. They expect them. They know that the risks and hardships ahead are nothing compared to the hardship they would have endured had they stayed where they were.

Margaret Arakawa, a young 29-year-old MBA marketing graduate said in a *Fortune* magazine interview, "Going to a place like P&G (Procter & Gamble) is out of the question. You'd be assistant to an assistant brand manager. If you got assigned to something mature, like Tide, you could spend a year deciding whether to change the thickness of a line on a box a fraction of a centimeter. I want to work on a project I can get excited about."

Margaret wanted a stimulating, creative environment where she could contribute and grow, not just collect a paycheck. Where did she go? To Microsoft.

Ambitious people want more than a job. They want something exciting, something new. Many are joining Web-based companies or launching businesses on their own. Many others would like to do something similar but don't know where to begin. The best place to start is letting your imagination go wild. Then have the guts to go where it leads you.

As Po Bronson, writer for the computer monthly, *Wired*, says in his book, *The Nudist on the Late Shift*,

"You don't have to be a genius.
You don't have to be superman.
You don't even have to be a techie.
Just have an idea."

All you need is a good imagination and you'll find fertile soil. And . . . the best ideas are right under your nose.

Ron Gordon, a native of Lima, Peru, arrived in the U.S. almost 30 years ago as a teenager. He became homesick for news of his favorite soccer team. Realizing that many other immigrants felt the same way, he let his entrepreneurial talents kick in, and he began a newspaper which listed the soccer scores.

Mr. Gordon expanded his work and filled a gap in the Latino community. He thought of all the Hispanic artists and television shows that he watched as a boy back home in Peru. Mr. Gordon ventured to work in the growing Hispanic news and entertainment industry and to create some of the first U.S.-produced television shows for the Latino community.

Mr. Gordon and his partner, Argentinean-born Eduardo Zavalda, made a pitch to a nationally syndicated TV show back in 1983. The rest is ZGS history . . .

In 1989, Mr. Gordon formed ZGS Broadcasting, Inc., which consists of Spanish television stations in Washington, D.C., and Orlando, Florida, as well as a Spanish radio station and television station in Tampa, Florida. The television and radio stations reach more than one million Hispanic people.

In 1997, ZGS Communications, Inc., and ZGS Broadcasting, Inc., had combined revenues of approximately $8 million. ZGS Communications was nominated for four Emmys and won two.

Some of the best ideas are right under your nose. With fertile soil, imagination, and guts, anything and everything is possible. These are the two ingredients that have been the keys to many an immigrant success story. With imagination and guts you can make it in America. Just ask Ignacio Villejas.

He had $20 in his pocket when he moved to the United States from Mexico. He came to study English, but his entrepreneurial instincts soon took over.

While attending night school, he opened a flower shop, Unique Flowers, in his garage. Fourteen years later, he had his own house, a booming business in San Jose, and the distinction of having one of his flower arrangements used at President Clinton's inaugural ceremony.

As parents, teachers, mentors, counselors, consultants, and heads of organizations, let's remember to help nurture *imagination and guts* in the minds of all.

It is our responsibility to recall and instill the immigrant ideals that were the cornerstones of our forefathers. Start with the imagination and guts that caused them to risk what they had in order to pursue a safer, better environment—the imagination and guts that it took to go from sea to shining sea, through parched deserts and rocky gorges in search of fertile ground.

Yes, to make it in America you need imagination and guts. And when coupled with those other old immigrant ideals of honesty, integrity, hard work, and caring, young and old alike can, like our immigrant parents, leave a lasting legacy.

If you want to *Make It in America*, remember . . .

- Keep your eyes open for the right opportunity.

- Have the guts to follow the road no matter where it leads you.

- The best ideas are right under your nose.

> Regret for the things we did can be tempered by time; it is regret for the things we did not do that is inconsolable.
> **—Sydney J. Harris**

Chapter 19

SELF-LEADERSHIP

(THE POWER OF ONE)

So what if life does throw you one of those totally devastating and unsuspecting curves? Does it mean that's it for you, you had your chance and you blew it? Does it mean the party is over? No! Success requires that we take a hard look at the cards life has dealt us and still find a way to win.

How many times have you heard these statements?

"I didn't get the job because I'm female?"

"He got the promotion because he is the boss's yes-man."

"I can't go back to school, I'm over 40."

As legitimate as these statements might be, they are nonetheless excuses. Immigrants, for the most part, are intolerant of excuses. They expect things to be tough, and they are prepared to make the necessary sacrifices.

Even if it means temporarily relying on assistance from family, friends, or the government, they keep fighting until they find a way to make it on their own. And seldom do they rely more on entitlements than they do on themselves.

Let me tell you the story of Sarian Bouma. She came here from Sierra Leone in 1974 to attend college. After a failed marriage, she was forced to leave college and accept welfare in order to take care of her infant son.

Living on welfare was not exactly the fulfillment of her American dream. She realized that she would never be able to properly take care of her son unless she took matters into her own hands. She started working at a variety of different jobs and saved enough to purchase a cleaning franchise in 1987.

Ms. Bouma began her company with one employee and a contract to clean 200 square feet of space. Five years later, in 1992, with the assistance from the U.S. Small Business Administration, she secured contracts for more square footage. Today she oversees an operation that cleans 2 million square feet of space, employs a staff of almost 200, and generates over $1,750,000 in annual sales.

Ms. Bouma was named the Small Business Administration's 1998 Entrepreneur of the Year at both state and national levels. She is also the recipient of the 1999 Immigrant Achievement Award, given annually to outstanding first-generation Americans and immigrants. The award recognizes contributions that have greatly enriched our nation, and that bring immeasurable benefits to all Americans.

Ms. Bouma's story illustrates what one can do with determination and self-leadership.

Her story doesn't end here. Ms. Bouma epitomizes what real success is all about. Genuine success goes beyond the accumulation of wealth to "heart gain" and embraces the joys of giving. Ms. Bouma has never forgotten the days when she too received welfare. She hires people who must rely on public assistance, who are homeless, and who came here as immigrants in an effort to help them start down the road to financial independence. Her vice president is a former welfare recipient, and last year 10 employees purchased their own homes.

And she is not alone. Female and male immigrants alike, whether high-tech or low-tech, college-educated or not, find ways to make it in America. Immigrants are not only self-leaders, but they bring fresh eyes and a fresh perspective to whatever they encounter. That was the point in an *Inc. Online* magazine article on the 1995 Entrepreneur of the Year runner-up, Jirka Rysavy.

In the article, author Stephen Solomon tells Rysavy's tale. Jirka Rysavy came to America in the mid-1980s as a Czech immigrant with no money, no understanding of capitalism, little knowledge of English, and no idea what to do next.

The article tells how Rysavy bought a small retail office supply business, not unlike millions of retail operations throughout America. But Rysavy never meant to stay small for long.

He sold the same staplers and steno pads as everyone else. What was different—very different—was that he'd figured out a far superior way of doing it.

Rysavy never had formal business training. In fact, even capitalism was new to him. "I knew nothing about business," he says. "In Czechoslovakia, private business was called 'illegal enrichment.'"

To better understand the specific problems he would face as a manager, Rysavy pored over every relevant book and magazine article he could find. "It was cornflake university—I learned from business articles I read over breakfast," he says. "I clipped articles. I wanted to know what mistakes were made by CEOs of growing companies. So I read articles to find the relevant answers, to get ideas to think about."

One of his neighbors owned an office-supply store in downtown Boulder, Colorado and wanted to sell it. In fact, the owner wanted to get out from under the debts he owed. The store seemed successful, grossing $300,000 a year in sales, but it was losing money. When Rysavy took a look at the business, the problems seemed not at all difficult to fix. He was able to acquire the store for an unbelievably cheap price, paying only $100 and assuming $15,000 in overdue accounts payable.

An article from a publication produced for the 1995 Entrepreneur of the Year competition, in which Rysavy was a runner-up, tells the rest of the story "When he took over, Rysavy installed a computer system to track customers and sales. It was obvious that sidewalk businesses could not pay the bills, but Rysavy was intrigued by a handful of successful accounts with local companies that bought office supplies in large quantities. To Rysavy, the future of the operation seemed obvious: Move away from retail sales and focus instead on the corporate side.

"Following that strategy, he says, he expanded sales nearly eight-fold to $2 million within one year, with a pretax margin of 14%. This quick success made him think, 'Could I do the same thing in multiple locations?'

"In the fall of 1987, Rysavy sought the answer. He hired a researcher to collect material on the office-supply industry. That December, he packed a pile of documents two feet high and went to Maui for two weeks of reading."

What Rysavy discovered in his reading was a huge industry riddled with inefficiencies. A few savvy merchants—Staples and Office Depot among them—had already begun to terrorize local dealers by opening superstores where they sold office products at discounted prices.

But superstores served mostly retail customers and small businesses. What Rysavy saw was an opportunity to do the same thing for midsize and large companies.

"Through his research, Rysavy found out that purchases by corporations with more than 100 employees accounted for $30 billion annually in the office-supplies market. By selling directly to those customers, instead of operating superstores catering to walk-ins, Rysavy was certain he could generate better returns on capital."

Corporate Express, Inc., is one of only 10 companies in the world to reach $3 billion in revenue in 10 years. It recently merged with Burhmann NV (Amsterdam: BUHR), a leading international business services and distribution company. The combination of these two premier organizations creates the world's leading business-to-business office supply and services company, with total revenues of approximately $9 billion, 30,000 employees, and operations in 28 countries.

One might think that Rysavy was just lucky—he was at the right place at the right time and followed through on a hunch. But that's not true. Rysavy started another company, Gaiam, in 1988 but Corporate Express took most of his time and attention. Once he got that up and running he returned his attention to Gaiam. It quietly ascended *Inc.* magazine's 500 list, reaching No. 11 in 1997 from its 34th spot the year before. Today it ranks No. 4 with 1998 sales of $30.805 million, a 13,352 percent increase in sales growth in the last five years. That's making it in any language.

Doing it twice is not luck. It's fresh immigrant eyes with moxie; it's plain and simple savvy business know-how!

There are many, many stories of savvy immigrant leaders. Some become entrepreneurs and stay entrepreneurs. Others seek out, or join, large prestigious firms in mainstream America. Some, like Dr. Jeong H. Kim, do both.

Dr. Kim founded Yurie, a high-tech communications equipment company, in 1992 while working as a senior project engineer at Allied Signal. Just five years later, *Business Week* named it "America's #1 Hot Growth Company." In May 1998, Lucent Technologies purchased Yurie for one billion dollars, and Dr. Kim assumed a key leadership position as president of the company's Carrier Networks Group.

He credits his seven-year career as a U.S. Navy officer with giving him the leadership skills, management skills, and sense of accountability necessary to grow and manage a company successfully. However, I believe Dr. Kim had leadership qualities in him long before he joined the Navy.

In 1975, at the age of 14, Dr. Kim came to the U.S. from Korea. Despite lacking proficiency in English, he maintained a grueling schedule, earning his undergraduate and graduate degrees while maintaining full-time jobs.

Like so many others, the immigrant spirit and desire drove Dr. Kim to follow and accomplish his dreams no matter what the obstacle.

If you want to *Make It in America*, remember . . .

- Become blind to excuses.

- Depend more on yourself than on others.

- Develop yourself and then teach others to do the same.

> While others may give support and help, the
> key to your success is YOU.

Chapter 20

COMPETITION

(IT'S ALL IN THE MIND)

I was startled by the voice over the intercom.

"Ladies and gentlemen, we have been cleared for landing at New York's John F. Kennedy International Airport."

My heart began to race uncontrollably. It was as if someone had shot a syringeful of drugs into my veins. Although my ears were clogged, as they are prone to be on flights, I could literally *hear* my heart beating. It was so intense, it scared me.

The rest of his announcement, "please return all seat backs and trays to their upright position," sounded faint and distant. I don't know how long I was lost in the trance. The next thing I recall was pressing my head firmly against the back of the chair as the tires on the plane slammed onto the runway. I heard that familiar voice say, "Welcome to New York."

My joy exploded! I'll never forget the feeling. I imagine it might be similar to the instant rush of emotion that comes when a new parent hears the words, "Congratulations, you have a healthy baby boy (or girl)."

I was in America. I was in New York City. Busy, fast-paced, crowded, competitive, noisy, overwhelming, intimidating, exciting, wonderful New York City.

This time was different. I had been here before on vacation, but this time, *I was here to stay*. Would this . . . could this . . . become home? I didn't know.

Still, I was here, and that was the only thing that was important.

Many business books steer entrepreneurs away from crowded markets, arguing that competition lowers the chance of success. But immigrants see things differently. We aren't looking for the whole pie, just a slice. "Lots of people" aren't seen as competition, but rather confirmation of fertile soil.

I'll never forget my first day in the city. It was a cool, crisp spring night, noticeably cooler than any night back in Jamaica. We were going to the legendary Radio City Music Hall.

I can still remember the theater. The splendor and richness of the deep crimson and gold decor was like nothing I'd ever seen, even in the movies. I could feel my face flush with childlike wonderment as the Rockettes danced and kicked with unbelievable symmetry. With each kick, my excitement seemed to rise. I felt as if I could literally burst. I knew I was in a very special place. It was not just the theater. I was caught in the magic of New York City, and the feelings were electric.

New York, or should I say Manhattan, is like no place else. And like America, it is full of contradictions.

It is crowded and frantic. Yet, smack dab in the middle of the city, there is Central Park, a huge park that, after a snowfall, is a picture of tranquility that could rival many New England towns.

In the middle of the gridlock of taxis, there are placid horse-drawn carriages with bells and tassels.

New Yorkers can be cold and impersonal, yet one minute later can be passionate, with that unmistakable "in-your-face" New York style. From Wall Street to Broadway, everything you encounter contributes to the contradiction that is New York.

In a city where many different ethnic groups and types of people coexist, the tendency to exclude what is different and to gather together what is homogeneous is seen everywhere. Take the subway to Greenwich Village, and you'll be absorbed into a young, trendy, eclectic, crowded, fun happening. Take a taxi to TriBeCa and you'll think you are in fashionably conservative London. Yet it is this living paradox, to separate yet tolerate, and to coexist with and co-mingle different values, that spawns the essence of America and the jewel that is New York.

It is this paradoxical quality that draws the optimist like a magnet. If there are lots of people, then there must be lots of opportunities. If there is that much diversity, then there is certainly a place for me. If there are ethnic neighborhoods, then surely I will be at home there.

As Frank Sinatra sang in the classic *New York, New York*, "If I can make it there, I'll make it anywhere."

New York is the most competitive city in the world.

But it is also the place with the greatest opportunity for those who have the optimism, passion, belief, and patience to "make it there."

And immigrants are by their nature eternal optimists. That is one of the reasons they come to New York City in droves. They know that old opportunities breed new opportunities. They are not afraid of competing in a metropolitan market of 18 million people. They know the more people there are, the more customers and the more opportunities there are.

If you want to find the immigrant spirit, you can find it best in the teeming, hustling, crazy New York City. And since the closing of Ellis Island, it is the John F. Kennedy International Airport that makes the heart pound. It has become the new entrance to the Promised Land—New York, the Big Apple in the new Garden of Eden.

If you want to *Make It in America*, remember . . .

* Think big.

* Don't fear competition.

* The more people there are, the more potential customers there are.

* The larger the market, the greater the opportunity.

The bigger the pond, the bigger the fish.

Chapter 21

PASSION AND PATIENCE

(YOU CAN NEVER HAVE ENOUGH)

Whether in love or in war, passion makes the difference. Without passion and patience, we will not have the stamina or fortitude to weather the challenges and changes necessary to be successful. And according to Tom Peters, "Within the next 10 years, we will witness the most fundamental and wide-reaching changes since the time of the caveman."

Think of the passion that immigrants must have to leave their homeland and everything else behind to start a new life. While beliefs are extremely important, it is the passion that takes beliefs into action. But passion also needs to be tempered with patience. That combination of passion and patience has helped many immigrants follow their dreams to ultimate success.

Ten years after arriving from Bangalore, India, Sabeer Bhatia, founder of the incredibly successful HotMail internet company, is the youngest and richest new entrepreneur of Silicon Valley. In an interview with *India Currents,* Bhatia said, "'This valley is a land of opportunities and this the place where legends are created every day. I wanted to start a company of my own and pursue some of my dreams.'" How did he do it? With imagination and loads of passion and patience.

Sabeer Bhatia had a good idea, but twenty different venture capital firms turned him down. However, he was not discouraged. He and his partner, Jack Smith, knew the power of passion tempered with patience.

In *The Nudist on the Late Shift,* Po Bronson tells how one night at a dinner gathering of The Indus Entrepreneurs,

Sabeer met Farouk Arjani. Back in the 1970s, Arjani had been a pioneer in word processing. These two Indian compatriots had much in common, and Arjani became Sabeer's mentor. Arjani commented, "What really set Sabeer apart from the hundreds of entrepreneurs I've met is the gargantuan size of his dream. Even before he had a product, before he had any money behind him, he had become completely convinced that he was going to build a major company."

And that he did. Sabeer Bhatia started HotMail in late 1995. Its vision was to offers free e-mail accounts that can be accessed anonymously over the Web. Two years later Microsoft acquired it for an estimated $400 million.

From the very start, passion coupled with patience has played a major role in this immigrant's success.

Bronson recalls, "One might have presumed that since Sabeer had been rejected by twenty previous [venture capitalists] and was virtually a nobody, he would be grateful to accept Draper, Fisher, Jurvetson's $300,000 on their terms. Tim Draper made the perfectly reasonable offer of retaining 30 percent ownership on a $1 million valuation. Sabeer held out for double that valuation—reducing Draper's cut to 15 percent. Their negotiation got nowhere, so Sabeer shrugged, stood up, and walked out the door . . . . His partner Jack says, 'I still can't believe he had the guts to walk out of that room.' His only other alternative was $100,000 in financing that Jack had arranged as backup from family and friends. 'If we'd gone that route,' Jack says, 'HotMail wouldn't exist today.'"

Repeatedly Sabeer showed maturity and wisdom as he held his ground and tempered his passion with patience over and over.

During development, the money dried up. But Sabeer was reluctant to ask for additional financing, reasoning that if he launched the service successfully first, he would have more leverage over investors. So he convinced his first fifteen employees to work for free with the promise of stock options.

"My greatest accomplishment," Sabeer says again and again in Bronson's book, "was not to build the company, but to convince people that this is their company. I showed people how this would ultimately benefit themselves. My role is that of an enabler. No individual made this happen. I didn't do the work. We initiated an avalanche."

Bronson notes, "By the time Sabeer went back to Doug Carlisle at Menlo Ventures to say he needed the money, HotMail had 100,000 subscribers. His ploy of stretching the money an extra two months increased the valuation by $18 million."

During his negotiations with Microsoft, passion and patience again played a major role. Bhatia admits he didn't know how to sell a company. But he did know how to buy onions. "In India you've got to negotiate for everything, even buying vegetables." So when the bargaining started, he felt right at home. "They came in low with $160 million, so I came in at $700 million! And when they said: 'That's ridiculous! Are you out of your mind,' I knew it was just a ploy."

When the offer doubled to $350 million, HotMail investors said, "Sell." Bhatia returned to the table, and once more said, "No." The contract was finally inked on December 30, 1997, Bhatia's 29th birthday. The price: some 3 million Microsoft shares worth $400 million. As of June 1999, those shares have doubled in value. However, HotMail users are signing up at the rate of 125,000 a day, and the firm is currently valued at some $6 billion.

Sabeer's latest brainchild is a new e-commerce portal project called Arzoo ("passion" in Hindi and "my desire" in Urdu). That's exactly what Bhatia and his team are eager to do, fulfill online shoppers' desires—with passion.

Passion, passion, passion, patience, patience, patience.

Whether you are an entrepreneur or an intrapreneur contributor, build the kind of company that will attract the brightest and the best, the kind of company where people not only want to come, but stay. Or as Jim Stuart, co-founder of the Leadership Circle, confirms, "Passion, creativity, and commitment are the qualities that companies need most if they want to win in the new world of business."

If you want to *Make It in America*, remember . . .

- Time is money.

- Passion takes beliefs into action.

- You need passion and patience to stay the course.

> "An idealist believes the short run doesn't count. A cynic believes the long run doesn't matter. A realist believes that what is done or left undone in the short run determines the long run."
>
> **—Sidney J. Harris**

Chapter 22

LEVERAGING ASSETS

(A HAND IS NO HANDOUT)

It is hard, if not impossible, to build a successful business single-handedly. Support is often needed from others, especially during those early uncertain times.

That is why networking is at the root of the survival and strength of many immigrants. There are countless examples of immigrants whose survival and success have been made possible through the help of their families and communities. Pooling resources and living in crowded quarters, immigrants help each other survive.

When starting businesses, they pool resources of dollars and labor. They even help each other send money to families left behind.

Many Americans remember the old days, when our neighborhoods had a sense of togetherness, a sense of belonging, and a sense of family. Children could play and eat at a neighbor's house, and at times were even disciplined there. Sad to say, but today we barely know our neighbors. We wave or say hi as we grab the mail, and then return to the seclusion and safety of our own homes.

No wonder we find it challenging to work in teams on the job. How can we effectively work in teams when as a society we have become distrustful of one other? How can we effectively work in teams when we value our independence and privacy so much? Even when it comes to our families, many can't wait to move away—across town or across states.

Immigrants show us that if we are to treasure, recapture, and nurture that which made us great, then we must treasure, recapture, and nurture our families and our extended families—our support network. We must reach out and be that helpful and friendly neighbor with or without the old-time "welcome wagon." Simple acts of kindness can do much to dispel fears and strengthen bonds of friendship.

Nature has several sterling examples of the benefits and power of coming together. One is the simple snowflake. Snowflakes are one of nature's lightest and simplest things, yet when combined together they can cause an avalanche, one of nature's most powerful forces.

The sequoia trees of California are another powerful example from nature of the benefits that can be had by coming together. From a tiny seed, weighing only 1/3000th of an ounce, sequoia trees can grow to 300 feet tall. Some have a circumference of over 100 feet. It would literally take about 17 men with outstretched arms just to encircle some of them. These facts, in themselves, would put the sequoia in a class by itself. But what is truly inspiring about sequoia trees is their root system.

It would be normal to expect trees that tall to have equally deep roots. However, just the opposite is true. Rather than having deep penetrating roots, the sequoia has very shallow roots, some even growing aboveground. Their roots extend horizontally, connecting with the roots of nearby trees to form a flat mat of roots. It is this *network*, this interlocking root system that provides support and strength for the mighty sequoia. Without one another's support, these giant trees could not survive.

Reaching out, joining forces, and leveraging assets have allowed the sequoias to enjoy sustained growth. United and linked in a strong support network, they have been able to withstand violent storms, as well as California's frequent and often devastating earthquakes, to become one of the world's oldest living things. Some sequoias live upward of 3,000 years.

Immigrants have long learned the power behind these extended support systems. They constantly leverage their assets in support of one another. It is important that we also learn to come together in support of one another.

When we see ourselves as one, we will act as one. We won't mistrust or second-guess one another, but will cooperate and collaborate willingly. We'll work together for the good of the whole not just at work, but also in every aspect of our lives.

You might be wondering how you could get, for example, access to financial resources without family or strong community ties? Well, one way is simply to form your own community or support group.

A support group can start with just two or three people with a common goal, pooling time, knowledge, or financial resources for the good of all. Many successful neighborhood groups, business organizations, and investment clubs have started just this way.

When it comes to leveraging assets, if we can come together like snowflakes or sequoia trees do, we will be a force unmatched and unstoppable. We will form synergistic organizations whose strength and success are the hallmarks by which others are measured.

We must also teach our children how to come together, to cooperate. We need to teach them to be cognizant and considerate of others, even in the simple things—not playing radios so loudly that they disturb the next person, not skateboarding in other people's driveways or on busy sidewalks, particularly where elderly people or children could get hurt.

Yes, when we can see ourselves as one, we will feel a sense of responsibility to one another. We will gladly leverage our different assets in support of one another. We will become a family—an extended family of Americans.

If you want to *Make It in America*, remember . . .

- There is strength in numbers.

- Simple acts of kindness can often dispel fear and strengthen bonds of friendship.

- A hand is no handout.

United we stand, divided we fall.

Chapter 23

STRATEGY AND ACTION

(BRAIN AND BRAWN)

Legend has it that when immigrants came to America, they had no idea what they'd find. This is both truth and myth.

While most immigrants could not conceive of the real America they confronted upon their arrival, they had read letters, made contacts, and learned much before they came. By the time they arrived, most had a strategy for what would happen once they got here.

That strategy, more than likely, went something like this:

- get to America
- find a place to live
- find a job
- make some money
- bring the rest of the family over
- make more money
- build on what we've earned

Simple. But not easy.

American folk wisdom also has it that immigrants are naturally entrepreneurial. The challenge of beginning life in a new country is analogous to starting a business and venturing forth, economically, on one's own. The proliferation of highly visible "niches," such as the Korean corner grocery and fruit stand or the Italian pizzeria, lends weight to the popular notion.

In every American census from 1880 to 1980, immigrants were found to be significantly more likely to be self-employed than natives. The most recent figures of the U.S. Commerce Department's census bureau show that receipts for minority-owned businesses increased by 128 percent, from $92.1 billion to $210 billion, between 1987 and 1992.

An analysis of immigrant behavior suggests why this happens.

Thuan Nguyen, chairman of the Vietnamese Chamber of Commerce in Santa Clara County, said, "Most immigrants come here, see the opportunities here, and they want to be a part of the American dream."

Households typically make the decision about emigrating on a collective basis. The family members who are "chosen" often have personal characteristics similar to those of entrepreneurs. Like entrepreneurs, they tend to be dynamic risk-takers, especially in the early stages, when information about the point of destination is incomplete and the likelihood of success uncertain.

Strategically, they determine whom to send and where to go, so as to maximize the household's earnings and minimize risk. Just like portfolio managers, they "invest" labor (and typically capital, in the form of family savings) across national and international borders, and re-invest and distribute the dividends.

Mr. Nguyen said, "My biggest achievement has been creating job opportunities for other immigrants." Many of his employees would not get a break elsewhere. They are from Vietnam, Thailand, and Cambodia, and he prides himself in training these immigrants to earn a living.

"We employ many newcomers here and we see a lot of success stories here. They make good money and develop more skills. And even if an immigrant is employing only other immigrants, they are still producing services for the community."

In addition, immigrant-owned businesses use other suppliers, assisting all those who work in connecting industries and thereby providing business for them as well. It has a rippling effect in the economy.

Another path many immigrants have used to make it in America is through real estate. Irving Howe, in his book, *World of Our Fathers*, recalls the investment strategy many immigrants used to obtain income-producing property on Manhattan's Lower East Side in the early part of the 1900s. Though the numbers have inflated, the description of how it happened remains unchanged.

> First they become lessees. By constant saving, the Eastsider gets together $200 or $300 with which, as security, he gets a four- or five-year lease of a house. He moves his family into the least expensive apartment. He himself acts as janitor, his wife and daughters as scrubwomen and housekeepers. He is his own agent, his own painter, carpenter, plumber, and general repairman. Thus he reduces expenses to the minimum.

> He lets out apartments by the week, always calling promptly himself for the rent. By thus giving constant attention to his work, he has perhaps a few hundred dollars every year as profit. By the time his lease expires, this has swelled to a few thousand. With this he buys a tenement outright. He puts from $3,000 to $5,000 down on a $45,000 building, giving one, two, three, sometimes four mortgages in payment. Then he repeats his old operation. When the third or fourth mortgage comes due, he has invariably made enough out of the building to pay it off. He keeps on, hard at work, and likewise pays off the third and second. Then, as his rents still come in, he invests them in more tenements; until, as a monument to a life spent in the hardest sacrificial toil, he may own a string of buildings scattered all over town.

In order to be a success, whether through real estate, a corner convenience store, technology, or some other medium, you need a long-range plan backed up with a myriad of tactical steps.

Yes, two critical factors for making it in America are strategy and action.

If you want to *Make It in America,* remember . . .

- To fail to prepare is to prepare to fail.

- You've got to have a plan.

- And you've got to stick to it!

> "All things come to him who hustles
> while he waits."
> **—Thomas Edison**

Chapter 24

THE WORKPLACE OF THE FUTURE

(IT'S HERE)

Soon we will all be "immigrants" in a new and unfamiliar world.

The world is changing, and nowhere is the world changing more than in the American workplace. Whatever our idea of what the workplace does look like, or should look like, it will be completely different before we know it.

I believe the workplace of the future will resemble a combination of Walt Disney's Epcot Center in Orlando, and the stock market's Standard and Poor's 500. Epcot is a center of social and ethnic diversity, creativity, customer service, and thriving capitalism. The S&P 500 features a diverse set of companies in a variety of sizes.

Similarly, I believe the workplace of the future will encompass companies and industries that include a large number of ethnic and regional cultures from all around the world, as evidenced by many of the multinational mergers like Daimler-Chrysler, Bank of America-Nation's Bank, and WorldCom-MCI. These companies have positioned themselves to take advantage of a wide range of experience and knowledge to compete domestically and globally.

Many multinationals feel that diversity gives them an advantage, since they get a more accurate read on customer and industry trends. For the same reason, many analysts consider the S&P 500 to be a more accurate benchmark for measuring the performance of the U.S. stock market than the Dow Jones average. The Dow is composed of just 30 large-capitalization, blue-chip stocks. In contrast, the S&P 500 includes a larger number of companies with a wider range of market sizes. Thus, the S&P 500 is able to take a more precise "snapshot" of the overall market's ebb and flow.

Operating units are getting smaller, flatter, and more entrepreneurial. Organizational charts have already begun to disappear in many companies, as employees find themselves reporting to multiple project leaders and cross-functional teams.

Additionally, organizations are forming global partnerships with the many outsourcing and contracting firms that are springing up like mushrooms. The workplace of the future is evolving quickly and is quite different from that of the bureaucratic corporate giants of the twentieth century.

It is here that we all become immigrants from one century to the next, moving into a business world that is not only different from what we have now, but one that is, and will continue to be, constantly changing.

So, this is a very appropriate time to reflect on the successes of immigrants, especially to capture their pioneering mentality, and to learn how they adapted and leveraged changes.

As we enter the 21st century, one of the biggest challenges facing American companies, entrepreneurs, and intrapreneurs will be how to create a passionate following among customers who have so many choices. The answer lies not in fearing the competition, but, like immigrants, focusing on strengths and not on weaknesses. Like immigrants, we cannot hide our differences, but rather must exploit them.

In business and marketing terms, exploiting one's strengths falls under the umbrella of branding.

When we think of branding, we think of industry leaders: Nike, Starbucks, and Coca-Cola. But what would you do if you had to compete with one of these giants? The answer is to pick your weapon carefully. Like David taking on Goliath or immigrants taking on New York City, you should use your imagination—and don't forget about strategy and guts.

Before Bob Pittman became president and COO of America Online, he worked for Six Flags, the amusement park giant. Who was his competition? Disney. He knew that if you want success, you don't compete. You differentiate.

Pittman focused on two key differentiators: Six Flags parks are not only larger than Disney parks, but they are found all across America. Therefore, they are within a day's drive of 90 percent of Americans. He began advertising Six Flags parks as "Bigger than Disney, closer to home." Once people understood the convenience Six Flags offered, park attendance quickly grew from 18 million visitors per year to nearly 25 million.

Pittman used good old immigrant qualities of imagination and guts, strategy and action, and lots of passion.

But what if you are just a struggling entrepreneur? Can you be equally successful competing against industry leaders? Once again, the answer is, "Don't compete. Differentiate."

Brian Mair, an immigrant from Jamaica, has a small entrepreneurial company that distributes electrical appliances. He provides appliances to the multihousing industry. His competition includes industry leaders such as Sears, General Electric, and Whirlpool. Brian used strategy, simple unbridled imagination with lots of guts, and taught the big boys a thing or two.

His strategy was threefold. To carve out a niche, he had to find out what would make life easier for customers, and then find a way to deliver it. The biggest headache for the multihousing industry with respect to appliances is getting new ones or replacements in the units quickly so they can maintain happy tenants.

Brian therefore established a division of his company to cater directly to their replacement needs. He called on these management companies and quickly differentiated himself from the competition.

His company, ARD Distributors, offered many advantages. They guaranteed next-day delivery, whereas the competition asked for a three- to seven-day window. ARD also believed in truly servicing its customers. The company offered to uncrate the appliance, deliver it to the unit, and take away the old appliance and packing materials. Their competition would simply drop off the appliances in the parking lot, leaving it up to the customers to uncrate, deliver, and dispose of everything themselves.

ARD Distributors has been extremely successful with this strategy. It has been so successful that now GE and Sears are attempting to offer similar services in order to stop further erosion of their business.

Whether you are a large corporation or a small entrepreneurial venture, being successful in the workplace of the future calls for catering to your customers and differentiating your services.

My favorite magazine, *Fast Company*, had its own predictions for what will be needed for success in the workplace of the future. It quoted Michio Kaku, author of *Visions: How Science Will Revolutionize the 21st Century*. Michio said, "Two things technology isn't good at: Computers don't have common sense and they don't have real vision. You just can't automate specialized human services."

Fortunately, these are precisely the two things most immigrants have, vision and loads of practical common sense when it comes to customer service.

In her book, *Thinking in the Future Tense*, Jennifer James has great advice for intraprenueurs. She notes that "your job and security will depend on your own competencies and work skills. That makes you responsible for staying on the cutting edge when it comes to skills development and knowledge of your business or profession and the market in which you compete."

What if you are the head of the company? How do you prepare the workplace of the future? Watch the trends and watch what immigrants do to make it in America.

When immigrants come to America, they come in search of better tomorrows. So they eagerly search for new frontiers and embrace the excitement of the unknown. They adopt American ways as their own and integrate their culture on top of it. Mentally, they prepare to stake their claim to a piece of the American pie.

People today want to work for companies they can identify with. They want to connect with more than a paycheck and a logo. They want to work where there is connection, an exchange and integration between the company's mission and principles and their own personal, emotional, and spiritual goals and values. They want better tomorrows.

Take a look at the huge exodus, of blue-chip executives, bankers, and lawyers from what were once considered dream jobs to go to Web start-ups. Why are they leaving? It's because both their companies and their industries have become complacent. Who wants to sit around year after year doing the same old thing? Sure, you can change the packaging like the thickness of a design line on a box of Tide, or the marketing, but virtually it's the same old thing. They want new challenges, new frontiers.

That was the thrust of a *USA Today* article by Thor Valdmanis on October 12, 1999, entitled, "Blue-chip execs wooed by Web start-ups." Brandyn Criswell, who left Wilson Sonsini for on-line news service Cnet, says: "I didn't do this because it's any easier. The difference is the passion and the sense of ownership, having a stake." Former Volpe banker Paul Werhley, who jumped to on-line search engine Ask Jeeves in March, added, "You're taking on a financial risk (only one in 10 start-ups succeeds), but it could pay off. It's also sexier than investment banking." The latest big executive to join the Web craze is Andersen Consulting CEO George Shaheen, who ditched a $3 million salary to join on-line grocer Webvan.

Entering the workplace in the 21st century will be like entering a whole new world. And you can have an advantage if you approach it with fresh immigrant eyes. Look to the future with hope and excitement. Bring to it your imagination and passion.

Stay in touch with your immigrant roots; embrace the unknown.

These common-sense, simple concepts and strategies that immigrants have used can help you amass not just financial success, but also a life with purpose and pride. Accepting and adopting these immigrant characteristics can prepare you for making it in the workplace of the future. After all, who deals with more massive change than the immigrant?

With core immigrant qualities and ideals—such as visions; belief in God, country and self; and personal passion and perseverance—everyone can make it in America.

If you want to *Make It in America*, remember . . .

- Couple social and ethnic diversity with creativity and size.

- Don't compete, differentiate.

- Integrate and adapt.

To conquer the future, embrace the unknown.

Chapter 25

THE UNCONSCIOUS PROCESS
(JUST DO IT)

There's no mistake about it: Making it in America is hard work. And since it is your hard work that will be put into achieving success, you must be in the driver's seat. If you are serious about achieving success, this is the only way to do it.

Whether employee, entrepreneur, or intrapreneur (a free agent within a company), success is not something that can be delegated or left to chance. You must become the president and CEO of your own enterprise. As Tom Peters would say, "become the CEO of YOU Incorporated."

You must take the leadership role in this venture. You must have the vision, and determine the markets and the strategy. You must also be ready to assume the risks, pay the price, and reap the rewards.

Miraculously, when you are ready, the process unfolds. If you were to ask most successful immigrants what process or methodology they used, chances are they couldn't tell you. This is because for many, it came instinctively, naturally. It wasn't until I sat down to try to put the steps I used into words that the actual process unfolded. I firmly believe that this process, in whole or in part, has played a role in the success of many, if not most, immigrant ventures.

Remember, immigrants for the most part approach most things from a very practical, common-sense point of view. So the process itself is simple.

The four cornerstones of the process are **DBA-P**. The first three letters stand for *Dreams, Beliefs,* and *Action.* These are the three main parts to the process. Some will try to get by with one or two of the three, but it seldom works. All three are needed.

Additionally, even if you have all three parts, you still need the fourth part, which is the glue that keeps the parts together. What is this glue? It is *Passion.* Let's run through the entire process.

Everything starts with the vision, the big *DREAM.* Dreams are the sparks that light the fire, which starts the whole process rolling. Think of dreams as the guidance systems of a rocket. For immigrants, their guidance systems are instinctively aimed at America, the place where dreams come true.

Dreams should be motivating, inspiring, and stimulating, or you will not be willing to undergo whatever hardships are necessary to achieve them.

Every successful venture, large or small, must have a clear vision of what it is all about. The vision must be detailed and vivid enough that you can literally see it. The president and CEO must also be prepared to take it beyond the initial dream into a definable vision that can be shared, if necessary, with others.

Dreams must be so compelling that they give birth to the glue, the *passion.* If your dreams and your goals aren't compelling enough to get you excited, they are not compelling enough to motivate anyone else. And it's a sure bet that you haven't started dreaming big enough.

Sad to say, but many dreams never make it past the dream stage. They forever languish in the realm of the blurred, the undefined, the *what-ifs,* and *one-day-I-mays.*

The next component in the process is *beliefs*. You must believe with all your heart that this is worth doing. Your faith and beliefs must be so strong that you believe the only thing that stands between you and success is time. In other words, you see yourself already in possession of your goal and you are simply waiting for everyone else (your investors, customers, suppliers, etc.) to come to that same realization.

When you believe *that* strongly, you will have the passion, guts, and tenacity to fight the fight. And that's where the *action* comes in.

When you believe *that* strongly, your emotions and passion will not be restrained. Competition and obstacles that would thwart a person of lesser stamina become mere inconveniences. Your energy and enthusiasm become contagious. You don't have to spend a lot of time recruiting followers; they will be seeking you out. Everyone wants to be with a winner.

Your energies will instinctively be directed and focused on discovering the right strategies and actions to bring your dream into reality. And your vision, in all its detail, will begin to unfold as you align and apply individual strategies and tactics.

The process, though simple, is not easy. So don't try to do it all alone. As we said before, we all need to have family and community as part of our life-team. The people who will be there when you lose, will also be there when you win.

They are your support system. Find like minds, kindred spirits and fellow believers. Form communities of your own. Seek the wisdom that comes from diverse backgrounds. Don't fear competition; defy it with your uniqueness.

Also bear in mind that each of the four cornerstones is important, and trying to short-circuit any of them could spell disaster. Remember, if you try to go straight from *dreams* to actions while your belief systems are still weak, you will invariably run into trouble. If you believe and take action, but fail to develop the passion and enthusiasm, you may soon tire out, or become bored.

The DBA-P process is a simple, yet powerful, common-sense approach that has worked time and time again for immigrants throughout the ages. If you dream of new frontiers, if you dream of new beginnings, then this process can help you achieve them.

So now you know what immigrants know: *If you want to make it in America, have big powerful dreams fueled by enthusiasm and passion. And couple them with strong support systems, beliefs and actions.*

If you want to *Make It in America*, remember . . .

- Dream, and dream big.

- Believe in yourself and surround yourself with people who believe the same way.

- Develop the passion and take action.

Achieving a dream begins with having a dream.

Chapter 26

ONE LAST THING...

(THE END)

There was a time when Americans feared nothing. They had pride, not just in who they were, but in what they did. Even during the hardest of times—the Depression era and World War II—Americans had pride, pride in their jobs and pride in themselves. They believed that times would get better, and they took responsibility for making it happen.

As we stand on the threshold of a new century, let's once again position ourselves to take the winners' circle. Master fear, imagine the impossible, and celebrate as we make it happen.

When all is said and done, whether you are an immigrant or a descendent of immigrants, rich or poor, tall or short, black or white, or anything in between, remember . . .

YOU CAN MAKE IT IN AMERICA

So start dreaming!

And in the words of Henry David Thoreau,

"Go confidently in the direction of your dreams!"

A WORD OF THANKS

I am also grateful for the insights, stories, and facts provided by the following resources used in compiling this book:

The New York Ellis Island Museum

The Statue of Liberty Foundation

The New York Public Library

The Commission on Immigration and Naturalization

Ellis Island, Gateway to the American Dream by Pamela Kilian and Pamela Reeves (Crescent Books, 1991)

A Land of Immigrants by David M. Reimers (Chelsea House Publishers, 1996)

Ellis Island by Georges Perec with Robert Bober (The New Press)

The Other Americans by Joel Millman (Viking, 1997)

World of Our Fathers by Irving Howe (Touchstone Book, Simon & Schuster Publishers, 1976)

Thinking in the Future Tense by Jennifer James (Simon & Schuster, 1996)

The Nudist on the Late Shift by Po Bronson (Random House, 1999)

From Chinatown: A Portrait of a Closed Society by Gwen Kinkead (HarperCollins, 1992)

The New Republic, April 13, 1998, article, "The Open Society" by Peter H. Schuck

Inc. magazine article, "The Melted Pot," by Marc Ballon. Issue: February, 1999, page 025

Columbia University Record—May 15, 1996—Vol. 21

"Home-Buying by Immigrants Will Boost Housing Market" by Marcus Franklin, © 1997 Cox News Service

The Business Journal, San Jose

"Immigrants make dreams come true—With what little they started with, they found success," by Sona Sharma

A profile of Entrepreneurs of the Year by Stephen D. Solomon

ON-LINE SITES USED

American Immigration Law Foundation   http://www.ailf.org

Immigration and Naturalization Services
http://www.ins.usdoj.gov

Immigrants live American Dream on America's highway
http://www.amarillonet.com

National Women's Hall of Fame   http://www.greatwomen.org

American Civil Liberties Union   http://www.aclu.org

Joan Lloyd   http://www.joanlloyd.com

U.S. News and World Report, Inc.   http://www.usnews.com

Northern Light   http://www.nothernlight.com

Google.com   http://www.google.com

Libraries for the Future   http://www.lff.org

The National Immigration Law Center   http://www.nilc.org

Joint Center for Poverty Research   http://www.jcpr.org

The Wire News from the Associated Press   http://wire.ap.org/

INDEX

ABOUT THE AUTHOR

Marcia Steele is a featured speaker, seminar leader, and consultant. She says she knew at an early age that "selling coconuts to tourists" was not in her future, so she emigrated from the West Indies and headed straight for Wall Street.

Her incredible journey as a consultant and speaker has taken her around the world, from Madrid to Bangkok, Melbourne to Hong Kong, and London to Tokyo, for industry leaders such as 3M, Coca-Cola, General Electric, and Procter & Gamble.

Marcia was educated internationally as well as at Hunter College in New York City and the Rochester Institute of Technology. She is a member of the National Speakers Association.

To Contact the Author

To contact Marcia Steele for speaking engagements or correspondence:

Steele Success Institute
3651 Peachtree Parkway, Suite E-344
Atlanta, GA 30024-6009
Telephone: (770) 813-9767
Fax (770) 813-9864

Books are available at quantity discounts on bulk purchases for premium, educational, fund-raising and special sales use. For details call (888) 783-3535 or www.SteeleSuccess.com.

Information Request / Order Form

Fax orders: (914) 835-0398.

Telephone orders: Call 1 (800) 431-1579.
Have your credit card ready.

E-mail orders: orders@SteeleSuccess.com.

Postal orders: Steele Success Institute, 3651 Peachtree Pkway, Suite E-344, Atlanta, GA 30024-6009, USA.

Please send more FREE information on:
❏ Speaking/Seminars ❏ Training ❏ Consulting
❏ Additional Books

Name: _____

Address: _____

City: _____ State: _____ ZIP:_____

Telephone: _____

E-mail address: _____

Sales tax: Please add 7% for products shipped to Georgia addresses.

Shipping and Handling:
U.S.: $5 for the first book and $2 for each additional book.

International: $9 for the first book and $5 for each additional book.

Payment:
❏ Visa   ❏ MasterCard

Card number: _____

Name on card: _____

Exp. date: _____